RAW 101

Better Images
with Photoshop and
Photoshop Elements

RAW 101

Better Images
with Photoshop® and
Photoshop® Elements

Jon Canfield

SYBEX®   San Francisco • London

Publisher: Dan Brodnitz

Acquisitions Editor: Bonnie Bills

Developmental Editor: Pete Gaughan

Production Editor: Leslie E.H. Light

Technical Editor: Ellen Anon

Copyeditor: Kathy Grider-Carlyle

Compositor: Maureen Forys, Happenstance Type-O-Rama

Proofreader: Nancy Riddiough

Indexer: Nancy Guenther

Book Designer: Franz Baumhackl

Cover Designer: Richard Miller, Calyx Design

Cover Photographer: Peter K. Burian, www.peterkburian.com

Library of Congress Card Number: 2005924244

ISBN: 0-7821-4432-2

To Ken and Erin: The best kids a parent could hope for

 # Acknowledgments

My beautiful wife, Kathy, has supported me throughout this project and all the others I have taken on. She inspires me to do my best and gives me encouragement when I need it most. Kathy, marrying you was the smartest thing I ever did.

I'd also like to thank my good friends who have offered advice and support: Tim Grey, Peter Burian, Ellen Anon, and Charlotte Lowrie. All of them are fine authors who took time from their busy schedules when I had questions.

A special thank you goes to Art Morris and Peter Burian for letting me use their wonderful images in this book. It takes a great deal of trust for a professional photographer to give their RAW files to someone, but Art and Peter did so without hesitation. Art is one of the premier wildlife photographers in the world, and he offers instruction and inspiration. Visit his website at www.birdsasart.com. Peter is a well-respected stock photographer and author; his website is www.peterkburian.com.

Thanks go to John Nack and Mark Dahm at Adobe, who were both quick to answer my questions on Camera Raw, and special thanks go to Thomas Knoll for writing Camera Raw—the subject of this book.

And thank you to all the people at Sybex who made this book possible and guided me through the project: acquisitions editor Bonnie Bills, who saw the possibilities and made this project happen (congratulations to Bonnie and her husband on their beautiful little girl Beatrix!); developmental editor Pete Gaughan, whose sharp eye and patience were invaluable; production editor Leslie Light for keeping me on schedule; copyeditor Kathy Grider-Carlyle for cleaning up my butchering of the English language; the staff at Happenstance Type-O-Rama; and proofreader Nancy Riddiough. A special thanks to Ellen Anon for her outstanding technical edit. If any mistakes are left in this book, you can be assured they came after Ellen was done!

Dear Reader,

Thank you for choosing *RAW 101: Better Images with Photoshop and Photoshop Elements*. This book is part of a new wave of Sybex graphics books, all written by outstanding authors—artists and teachers who really know their stuff and have a clear vision of the audience they're writing for. It's also part of our growing library of truly unique digital imaging books.

Founded in 1976, Sybex is the oldest independent computer book publisher. More than twenty-five years later, we're committed to producing a full line of consistently exceptional graphics books. With each title, we're working hard to set a new standard for the industry. From the paper we print on, to the writers and photographers we work with, our goal is to bring you the best graphics books possible.

I hope you see all that is reflected in these pages. I'd be very interested to hear your comments and get your feedback on how we're doing. To let us know what you think about this, or any other Sybex book, please visit us at www.sybex.com. Once there, go to the product page, click the Submit a Review link, and fill out the questionnaire. Your input is greatly appreciated.

Please also visit www.sybex.com to learn more about the rest of our graphics line.

Best regards,

DAN BRODNITZ
Publisher
Sybex Inc.

About the Author

Jon Canfield is a landscape and nature photographer living in the Pacific Northwest, where he's blessed with some of North America's most scenic landscapes. He has been involved with digital imaging from its early days and has spent several years working on digital imaging software with Microsoft. Jon's articles and images have been published in *Shutterbug*, *PC Photo*, *Digital Image Pro*, and *PHOTOgraphic* magazines, among others. He recently co-authored *Photo Finish: The Digital Photographer's Guide to Printing, Showing, and Selling Images*, also published by Sybex (2004).

Foreword

Sometimes it seems like giving good advice is remarkably easy. Just offer the conservative recommendation, and you're pretty safe. This certainly holds true when offering photographic advice. Use a tripod. Use mirror lockup. Use a cable release. And of course, digital cameras have provided us with the latest addition to the long list of "safe" recommendations for photographers: Capture in RAW. The common thread among all these, of course, is that if you follow the recommendations, you'll achieve images of higher technical quality on a more consistent basis.

The problem is, although most photographers can very easily set their digital camera to capture in RAW, they don't understand how to best deal with those RAW captures to achieve their ultimate goal: producing the best images possible.

Fortunately, you hold in your hands the solution to this problem. *RAW 101* by Jon Canfield is an excellent book that—in plain English—explains everything you need to know to make the most of RAW capture after the picture has been taken. In addition to detailed coverage of how to convert your RAW images with both basic and advanced techniques, Jon shows you how to download the images to begin with, get them organized, and then put the finishing touches on your RAW captures after conversion to get them ready for printing. He even demonstrates how you can automate the process of converting a large number of RAW captures quickly and easily when speed is your primary objective.

RAW capture enables photographers to exercise unprecedented control over their images, and I think that is a truly exciting thing. For many photographers, working in a wet darkroom wasn't an attractive option, so they gave up much of the control over the final interpretation of their image. The digital darkroom has enabled photographers to have that control (and so much more!) again, all in the comfort of their computer chair. But RAW takes this control far beyond what was possible before. With it, we can now fine-tune the color temperature, extract maximum detail from shadow and highlight areas, and work with confidence using high-bit data to ensure the best quality possible in the final result—and Jon will guide you through all these topics in this book.

I think most photographers have become familiar with the concept that RAW capture can help them achieve the best quality. With this book, you'll go beyond the theory and learn to process your RAW captures with skill and confidence. And if you had any concerns about the complexities involved with RAW capture, let me put your mind at ease. I am fortunate enough to know Jon personally, and I can tell you that reading this book is just like having a conversation with him over lunch: comfortable and educational. You're in for a treat, and you'll be amazed at how much better your images can really be!

—Tim Grey
    Photographer, teacher, and author or coauthor of seven books on digital imaging, including *Color Confidence: The Digital Photographer's Guide to Color Management*

Contents

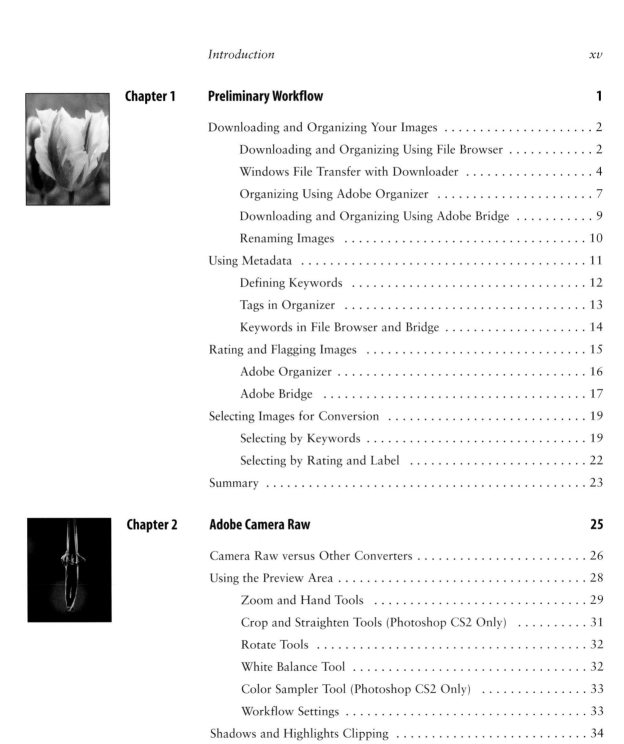

Chapter 5   **Automating Camera Raw**   **87**

Chapter 6   **Advanced Conversion Options**   **105**

"This book is all about giving you the information you  need to make RAW work for you now."

Introduction

It's hard to pick up a digital photography magazine or read a camera review these days that doesn't refer to the RAW file format. Since you've picked up this book, you are obviously interested in what the RAW format can do for you as well. This introduction explains the differences between RAW and other common formats, such as JPEG, and why RAW will give you superior results from your digital images.

What Is RAW?

A RAW file is the digital equivalent of a film negative. As with film, the RAW file contains information on the amount of light that was seen by the sensor. It knows nothing of how you intended the scene to be captured or what lighting was used. You retain control over how the RAW file is processed just as you would with a film negative.

Every digital capture begins as a RAW file, but when you select JPEG as the output, the camera's built-in RAW converter processes the file, applying the white balance, color correction, and compression settings according to the camera settings. It also converts your file to 8 bits per pixel, throwing out a good deal of color information that can be used for more control when editing the image; I'll cover that a little later.

In its most basic form, a RAW file is simply a collection of the luminance values recorded by each photosite at the time of capture, along with data containing the camera settings, and most likely a JPEG thumbnail that is used for review on the camera LCD.

Although RAW files are technically just the recorded value of light from each photosite, every camera manufacturer interprets this data differently, even when the same imaging sensor is used. This has led to the proliferation of RAW conversion programs, from independent companies as well as each of the camera manufacturers. The most popular option for many, though, and the subject of this book, is Adobe Camera Raw.

Note: Most of the sensors in use today come from a relatively small number of companies. Sony and Kodak supply a number of CCD imagers that are used in other cameras such as Nikon, Canon, Konica-Minolta, and Olympus. Fuji and the Canon CMOS cameras are exceptions to this, using sensors developed for their own use.

There are ongoing talks of standardizing the RAW format, but the chances of this happening in the foreseeable future are slim at best. With Adobe's creation and release of DNG specification, or Digital Negative, the likelihood that standards may become a reality is increased.

One of the key advantages to the DNG format, aside from Adobe's influence in the digital imaging market, is that your RAW files will be convertible in the future, even if you've replaced your digital camera with a different brand or if support for your camera's RAW format is discontinued.

Why You Should Shoot RAW

When total control and the highest possible image quality are needed, RAW is the perfect format to use. The greater dynamic range, color depth, and post-capture editing capabilities make the RAW format the best choice in most situations.

RAW files shouldn't be seen as the lazy person's way to great images, though. A poorly composed image, an out-of-focus image, or one with gross exposure errors isn't going to be magically transformed into a quality photograph just because you were able to edit the RAW file. It's still the responsibility of the photographer to get the best possible image *at the time of capture.*

 Note: RAW files give you more latitude and possibilities in the post-capture editing phase. But don't be lulled into thinking that RAW will save the day. Learn your camera, meter correctly, and capture with the same care you gave to film. Remember: "garbage in, garbage out" still applies in the digital world!

Advantages over JPEG and TIFF

RAW files free the photographer from having to be satisfied with what the camera thinks are the correct values for sharpening, noise reduction, and white balance. The differences can be startling! Since this information is all stored in addition to the file, it becomes possible to make changes to them after the fact. This is where the RAW format becomes so valuable.

When shooting in JPEG, the camera processes the color values based on the current white balance setting in the camera to create a final image. The file is then compressed to save space, using the camera's current quality setting. RAW capture, on the other hand, does no color interpretation in-camera, but depends on the RAW converter software to handle this task. Hence, you have much more freedom after the capture to either fine-tune the image or make corrections to basic problems such as an improperly set white balance.

RAW is the only capture method that preserves the full color fidelity of the image. With JPEG, you immediately throw away a third of the color information in your image. The sensor in most cameras records data as a 12-bit file, giving each pixel one of 4,096 levels of color. In order to take advantage of this, you'll need to shoot in RAW mode. JPEG only supports 8 bits per pixel, reducing the possible colors to 256 per pixel. It's easy to see that you'll record a more accurate representation of the subject with 4,096 choices than with 256! Less color information means that you have less latitude when editing the image for final output.

Also, JPEG is a *lossy* compression method: Every time a file is saved in the JPEG format, it loses a little more fidelity.

Note: Even in those instances when JPEG is the better option for your shooting, always save the file as a TIFF before doing any editing. This will avoid further compression and data loss from your image.

JPEG and TIFF also apply sharpening and noise reduction at the time of capture. If you've set these incorrectly and don't catch the error, you have little choice in the edit phase. The camera does not know what my intended use for an image is, and I don't believe it should ever be allowed to choose the sharpening or noise reduction it "thinks" I want.

Saving in camera as TIFF (Tagged Image File Format) is becoming much less common in recent cameras. Although some models (such as the Canon D-SLRs) tag their RAW files as "TIFF," these are not true TIFF files. TIFF is a standard file type for bitmap, or raster, data. Unlike JPEG, TIFFs are not subject to lossy compression or limited to only 8 bits of color information. The file sizes are large; a 16-bit TIFF file will be about three times the size of the same RAW file, because TIFF is saved at 16 bits rather than the 12 bits recorded by the camera. The extra bit depth is an advantage over JPEG, but the same control issues that JPEG suffers from are present in TIFF capture as well. Color balance, sharpening, and noise reduction are all applied directly to the image at the time of capture. The only advantage the TIFF offers over JPEG is color fidelity and lossless compression. To be honest, I can't think of a single instance where saving as a TIFF file in camera is a good option.

Note: TIFF is saved as a 16-bit file even though the sensor is only recording 12 bits of color information. The extra 4 bits of memory per pixel increases the file size dramatically because you're now saving 32,768 levels for each pixel rather than the 4,096 recorded by the sensor—but you're not getting more real information, just more file size. You get the same color advantage by saving as RAW and converting to 16-bit TIFF in the RAW converter.

When RAW Isn't the Best Choice

In a book about RAW image editing, it might seem a little odd to tell you that RAW isn't always the best choice. However, there are times when the extra work involved with RAW processing can't be justified. As an example, photojournalists typically shoot in JPEG when shooting for assignments. The image files are smaller, which is important for quick transfer to the newsroom, and the JPEGs can be used with little or no extra work before publishing. The JPEG format is also a better choice for event photographers, who may shoot (for example) youth sports events and want to make prints for sale right at the site. This is another case of speed being more important than ultimate quality.

Elements or Photoshop: Which is Right for You?

RAW 101 uses Adobe Camera Raw, which comes in two flavors. Photoshop Elements 3 is the first version of Adobe's popular entry-level imaging program to include support for RAW files and 16-bit images. The version of Camera Raw included with Elements is based on the one included with Photoshop CS. Some advanced features have been removed, and Auto settings have been added to assist with common image conversion options.

Photoshop CS2 has a whole new version of Camera Raw that, while keeping the same basic interface, has added features to make it more capable than ever, especially for batch processing and advanced exposure correction. I'll cover all of these features and differences. Table I.1 shows the major feature differences between the two versions of Camera Raw.

▶ **Table I.1** Adobe Camera Raw Feature Comparison

	Photoshop Elements 3	Photoshop CS2
16-bit output	Yes	Yes
Save custom settings	No*	Yes
White Balance tool	Yes	Yes
Preset white balance	Yes	Yes
Temperature adjustment	Yes	Yes
Tint adjustment	Yes	Yes
Exposure adjustment	Yes	Yes
Shadows adjustment	Yes	Yes
Brightness adjustment	Yes	Yes
Contrast adjustment	Yes	Yes
Saturation adjustment	Yes	Yes
Sharpness adjustment	Yes	Yes

▶ **Table I.1** Adobe Camera Raw Feature Comparison *(continued)*

	Photoshop Elements 3	Photoshop CS2
Luminance smoothing	Yes	Yes
Color noise reduction	Yes	Yes
Rotate image	Yes	Yes
Resize image	No	Yes
Crop image	No	Yes
Straighten image	No	Yes
Color samplers	No	Yes
Shadow/highlight clipping	Yes	Yes
Batch processing	No**	Yes
Color spaces	No	Yes
Resolution	No	Yes
Chromatic aberration	No	Yes
Vignetting	No	Yes
Curves	No	Yes
Calibration	No	Yes

* The Photoshop Elements version of Camera Raw only includes saving settings for Camera Default.

** Photoshop Elements requires separate steps to apply settings and convert.

So which should you use? The answer is simpler than you might expect. If you are just getting started with digital imaging, I recommend starting out with Photoshop Elements. Not only does it include most of the functionality of Photoshop CS2, it does so with an interface that's easier to use and learn and at a much better price.

If you already own Photoshop CS2, or are planning to upgrade to CS2 from an earlier version of Photoshop, then this is the obvious choice for you.

If you own neither but know that you will be shooting and processing large numbers of RAW image files, I recommend Photoshop CS2 for the extra flexibility in the Camera Raw converter and its integration with Bridge, the new file management program included with CS2.

Regardless of which version you choose or start with, the basic editing options are very similar. Where there are differences between the two versions, I'll call those out for you. If you find that these differences include features that you want or need, then it's time to upgrade to Photoshop CS2.

Who Should Use This Book

RAW 101 is for any digital photographer who is interested in going beyond the preset options in their camera and is ready to take control over the creative process.

If you have read about RAW capture, or tried it yourself and ran into the roadblocks that most of us did at the start, this book is all about giving you the information you need to make RAW work for you. You don't need to be a Photoshop Elements or Photoshop expert. In fact, if you have basic familiarity with either of these programs, you're ready to go. All you really need is a camera that captures RAW files and a copy of Elements or Photoshop with Camera Raw.

Throughout the book I'll show you how to get the most detail possible from your RAW files, whether it's correcting shadow and highlight detail, fixing white balance problems, or getting rid of noise.

In other words, if you were interested enough in learning about RAW to pick up this book, then you've come to the right place. I've sought to present the topics in a clear and easy-to-understand manner that focuses on results, not technology. If that sounds like you, let's get started!

What's Inside

Chapter 1: Preliminary Workflow presents essential techniques. These are the tasks that get your images ready for RAW file conversion.

Chapter 2: Adobe Camera Raw explores the CR workspace, what the controls are, and how they work on your RAW images.

Chapter 3: RAW Conversion covers the edits that will be done to almost every RAW file you process.

Chapter 4: Beyond the Basics shows you how to go beyond the universal tasks.

Chapter 5: Automating Camera Raw covers how to set up Camera Raw for "hands-free" operation to optimize your workflow when converting multiple RAW files.

Chapter 6: Advanced Conversion Options is about conversion options for Photoshop CS2 users.

Chapter 7: Finishing Touches covers the final tasks you'll commonly perform after converting your RAW images.

The **Appendix** provides a complete list of all the keyboard shortcuts available while you're working within Camera Raw.

How to Contact the Author

I love to share information on digital imaging and photography, and I hope that this book reflects that passion. I'd love to hear from you with comments about the book or to share your digital photo experiences. I can be contacted through jon@joncanfield.com, or visit my website at www.joncanfield.com.

Sybex strives to keep you supplied with the latest tools and information you need for your work. Please check their website at www.sybex.com for additional content and updates that supplement this book. Enter the book's ISBN—**4432**—in the Search box (or type **raw 101**), and click Go to get to the book's update page.

Preliminary Workflow

Shooting digital typically means dealing with large numbers of files. By taking the time to do basic organizational tasks and selections, you can reduce the amount of work required to go from shooting session to finished images. In this chapter, I'll cover ways to make managing digital files easier and less time consuming.

Chapter Contents
Downloading and Organizing Your Images
Using Metadata
Rating and Flagging Images
Selecting Images for Conversion

Downloading and Organizing Your Images

Before you can begin converting your images, you need to get them onto your computer. Mac users can utilize the Macintosh Image Capture application to handle this, while Windows users of Photoshop Elements can use the Organizer and Downloader. Either of these platforms will recognize when a camera or memory card is connected to the computer and automatically start, making the first step as easy as possible. If you're using Photoshop on either platform, Bridge can be used to copy images and organize them.

Because the Macintosh and Windows platforms handle file transfer so differently, I'll cover them separately throughout the book in these situations.

Although you can transfer images directly from your camera through a USB or FireWire connection, I prefer to use a card reader or external storage device for a couple of reasons. First and foremost, transferring directly from your camera means using a power supply or the camera battery. Hooking up a separate power supply is inconvenient, and using battery power means recharging sooner. Regardless of the power source, it also means no more shooting until the transfer is completed. I tend to shoot with multiple memory cards and travel with a laptop or battery-powered storage device for quick edits. This allows me to upload images from one card while I continue to shoot using another card. Of course the easiest method is to carry enough memory cards that running out of space isn't a concern. And, with the continuing drop in prices, this is becoming a realistic option for many of us.

Which application should you use?

- If you're using Photoshop Elements on Windows, I recommend using the Downloader application along with Organizer.

- Macintosh users of Photoshop Elements will be best served by using File Browser.

- If you're using Photoshop on either platform, I recommend using Bridge to handle your file copies.

Note: Windows users may want to try Downloader Pro from Breeze Systems (www.breezesys.com). This is a fast and full-featured application that can copy images, rename them, and add keywords. If you're looking for a faster solution, I highly recommend Downloader Pro.

Downloading and Organizing Using File Browser

Adobe File Browser (Figure 1.1) is available to both Windows and Macintosh users of Photoshop Elements 3 and Photoshop CS. Photoshop CS2 has replaced File Browser with the more powerful Bridge application.

The Mac and Windows versions of File Browser have some differences that make a single description of how to use it difficult to write. The Macintosh version of Photoshop Elements File Browser, perhaps to compensate for not having Adobe Organizer, has been beefed up from previous versions and is now the same as the File Browser included with Photoshop CS.

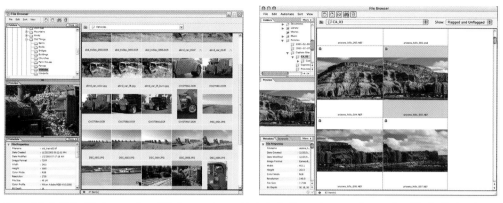

Figure 1.1 (left) The Windows version of File Browser does not include the Flag or Automate features found in the Macintosh version. (right) The Macintosh version looks very similar, but it includes a Flag files feature and the ability to add Keywords.

File Browser is where, on the Macintosh version of Photoshop Elements, you'll add keywords and mark files for editing or deleting. File Browser also contains the search function to help you find the image you are looking for among the hundreds or thousands on your computer.

With both platforms, File Browser can be used to copy images from memory cards to your hard drive. Begin by launching Photoshop Elements and selecting File > Browse Folders.

1. In the Folders panel, select your memory card and the folder that contains your images. In my example from the Macintosh, shown in Figure 1.2, this would be EOS_DIGITAL:DCIM:100EOS1D.

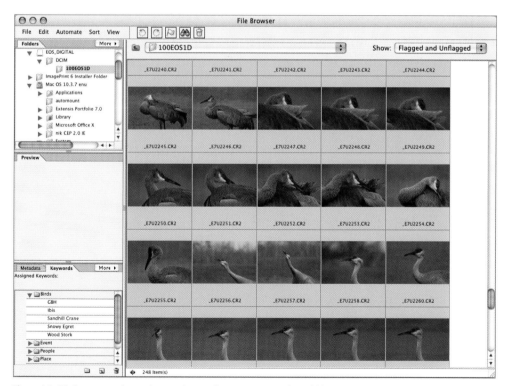

Figure 1.2 File Browser can be used to copy images from a memory card to a folder on your computer.

Note: Although iPhoto 5 or later can also be used to copy RAW files, I prefer to use File Browser. This lets me do all of my work in one application.

2. After selecting all the images on the card, choose Automate > Batch Rename. Select the Move To New Folder button and click Choose.

3. Select the folder you want to copy the images to, or create a new one. For my example, I've created a new folder named Florida in my Pictures folder.

4. Switch to the destination folder and give your files a descriptive name (see "Renaming Images" later in this chapter for suggestions on file naming), and click OK (Figure 1.3).

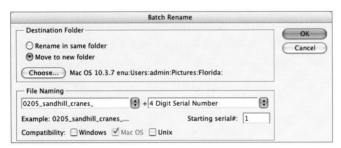

Figure 1.3
By using Batch Rename to copy images from a memory card to the computer, you can save a step later in the workflow.

Note: I've used Batch Rename to copy files for simplicity. It allows me to create a new folder on the fly, and it also renames the images as they are copied, saving me a step later in the workflow. You could also just drag the files from your memory card to a folder on your computer. This second method is faster at copying files but will require editing as a separate step later. I suggest trying both methods and seeing which works best for you.

Windows File Transfer with Downloader

Windows users have the same File Browser options as the Macintosh version of Photoshop Elements; however, Adobe Organizer, which is included with the Windows version of Photoshop Elements, adds the very useful Adobe Downloader program (Figure 1.4) to help get your images out of the camera and onto the computer. Downloader recognizes a device, whether it is a memory card or camera, when plugged into the computer.

To get started with Downloader, connect your camera or insert the memory card into a card reader. Downloader will read and display thumbnails of all the images found on the device. You can then select which images you want to transfer from the device to your computer, which can then be selected or excluded from transfer.

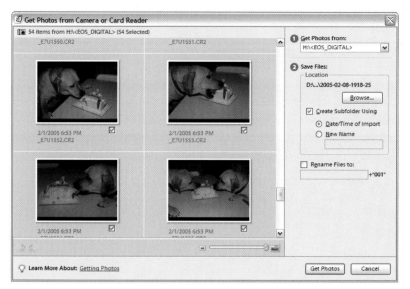

Figure 1.4 Transferring files on Windows is made easier with the Adobe Downloader, part of Photoshop Elements 3.

If Downloader does not start automatically, open Organizer and select Edit > Preferences > Camera or Card Reader. Make sure the option "Use Adobe Photo Downloader to get photos from Camera or Card Reader" is checked, as shown in Figure 1.5.

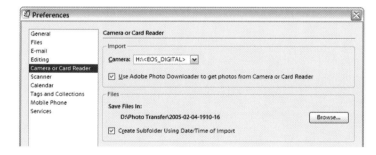

Figure 1.5

If Downloader doesn't start when your card or camera is connected, check the Preferences setting in Adobe Organizer.

When Downloader reads the device, all images will be selected for transfer. Using the checkbox below each thumbnail, you can uncheck any image that you don't want to copy to the computer (Figure 1.6). This can save some time when there are images that are obviously not worth further review.

Note: Many photographers will do at least a quick review in-camera during a lull in the action and delete inferior images at that time. This not only saves time when transferring images to the computer, but it also frees up space on the memory card for more shooting.

To help make the decision easier, Downloader has a slider to change the size of thumbnails (it's fun to play with too if you're as easily amused as I am) located at the lower-right side of the preview window. On the lower-left side are two buttons to rotate images.

Figure 1.6 By default, Downloader will transfer all images on a card. To avoid this, uncheck the box below any image you do not want transferred.

 Note: Although you won't be able to see as many images on screen, I recommend using the largest thumbnail size possible to help select which images to copy.

Once you have selected the images to transfer, the next step is to tell Downloader where to place them on your computer. The Save Files area lets you specify where you want the images to be copied and will create a new directory for each transfer. By default, these folders will be created using the date and time of import. Optionally, you can select the New Name radio button for a custom folder name (Figure 1.7).

Figure 1.7
You can rename the folder Downloader will use when copying images. This can save time later when you are sorting images, and it can make finding new files easier.

When shooting with multiple subjects, I recommend using the Date/Time Of Import setting to keep your images sorted. If I have several different subjects on the same card, this presorts them for me according to capture. If all the images being transferred are of the same subject, selecting New Name will allow you to save a step later.

Finally, the Rename Files To option lets you change from the default camera name, typically something like DSC02881, to a more human friendly name that has some real meaning, like "puppy_birthday." File names are appended with a sequential number to keep them unique. I prefer to name by date and subject, so in my example here, files would become 050201_puppy_birthday_001, 050201_puppy_birthday_002, and so on.

> **Note:** Using the rename feature means that each directory can have no more than 1,000 files using the same starting name. This should be more than sufficient though for almost any situation.

Organizing Using Adobe Organizer

Adobe Organizer (Figure 1.8) is only included with the Windows version of Photoshop Elements. Organizer is essentially a built-in version of Photoshop Album 2 with the same searching and organizing features as Album, including tagging, ranking, and sharing.

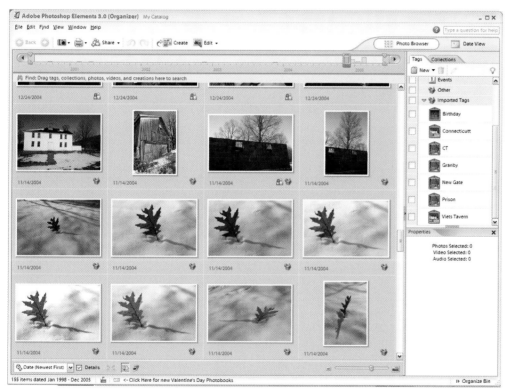

Figure 1.8 Organizer is included with the Windows version of Photoshop Elements and is a full-featured image manager.

> **Note:** For complete coverage of all the features contained in Organizer, I recommend *Photoshop Elements 3 Solutions* by Mikkel Aaland (Sybex, 2004).

Organizer makes tagging and finding images simple and relatively painless. Images can be grouped into Collections, which are a good way to organize images of different subjects that are in some way related. As an example, you might create a Summer Vacation collection that contains a variety of images from different sites that don't lend themselves to shared keywords.

Unlike File Browser or Bridge, Organizer only displays images that have been imported, either from a card, camera, or other source. If you have images already on your computer, you can add them to your catalog by selecting File > Get Photos > From Files And Folders (Figure 1.9).

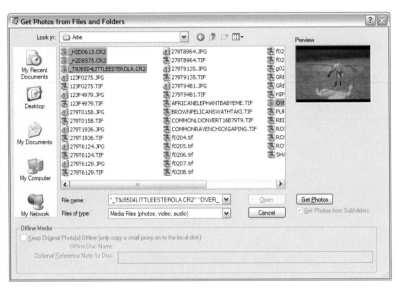

Figure 1.9 To import images already on the computer into Organizer, use the Get Photos dialog.

After selecting the files or folders to import, click the Get Photos button to begin importing images. Organizer will display a progress dialog showing each of the images imported.

Organizer, like most image management programs, doesn't actually copy the files. It creates a thumbnail of the image. When you select this thumbnail for editing, Organizer goes to the original file and opens it.

When importing into Organizer, only the images just imported will be displayed in the thumbnail window, which makes tagging much easier. Once you've finished tagging or rating images, click the Back To All Photos button just above the thumbnails display in Organizer to display all images in your catalog.

Note: If your images already contain metadata, Organizer will offer to import those tags along with the images. For some reason that must make sense to someone, the tags are imported but not actually applied to the images. You'll have to do that yourself after importing by selecting the tags and applying them to the images.

Downloading and Organizing Using Adobe Bridge

With the release of Photoshop CS2, the File Browser has been replaced with Bridge (Figure 1.10). Bridge works with all of the Adobe CS2 applications and adds the ability to view your images in more detail than you can in File Browser with a Filmstrip view that devotes most of the display area to larger previews of single images. You can also rate them for quality and apply labels to help you find the images you're seeking. Bridge also offers a nice Slideshow view (Figure 1.11) that can be used for displaying images or editing. Select View > Slideshow to begin. Images can be rated, labeled, or just viewed.

Figure 1.10 Bridge is a new feature included with Photoshop CS2 that replaces File Browser. Image rating and keywords are easy to apply and use for searching.

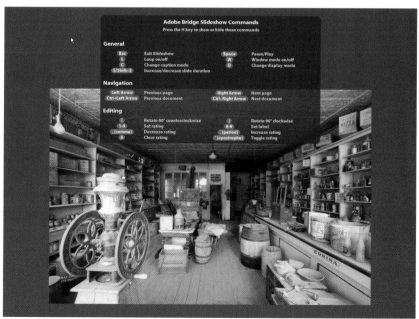

Figure 1.11 The Slideshow View in Bridge can be used to browse images as well as rate or label them.

Bridge looks very similar to the File Browser, but it has several new features that help make this a full-featured image manager, including Ratings, Labels, and the ability to do RAW image processing.

Like File Browser, the Folders, Preview, and Metadata panels are on the left side of the window. Bridge adds a Favorites tab to the Folders panel, making it easier to get to your files (Figure 1.12) by placing frequently used folders in your Favorites list. To add a folder to your Favorites list, select it in the Thumbnails panel and drag it to the Favorites panel.

Figure 1.12 Folders and Favorites help you find your images quickly in Bridge. To add folders to your Favorites list, drag and drop the folder onto the Favorites panel.

The feature set of Bridge is too large to cover in this book, but if you use Photoshop, it's worth taking a look at Bridge for your image management needs.

Note: For detailed information on Bridge, I recommend *Photoshop CS2 Savvy* by Stephen Romaniello and Matt Kloskowski (Sybex, 2005).

To copy files with Bridge, begin by launching Bridge and selecting the Folders panel.

1. In the Folders panel select your memory card and the folder that contains your images.

2. Select the folder you want to copy the images to, or create a new one. (See the earlier topic, "Downloading and Organizing using File Browser," for suggested naming methods).

3. Drag the files from your memory card to the new folder on your computer.

Renaming Images

Establishing a standard naming system will do more to help the initial workflow than almost anything else you can do. As I mentioned earlier when talking about image transfer, the name your camera assigns to an image is less than intuitive. Now imagine browsing through thousands of images with names like _E7U2349.CR2 or DCS22893.NEF, and you can easily see the benefit of giving your images a more understandable and memorable name.

Luckily, Photoshop Elements and Photoshop both make the renaming process painless. Elements has a Batch Rename function that can be found in File Browser. On Windows, select File > Rename Multiple Files. Macintosh users will select Automate > Batch Rename.

> **Note:** Organizer does not allow you to rename files. You'll need to use the File Browser to handle this task.

When renaming images you have the option to rename the file in the same folder, or to move the file to a new folder. Unless you have a reason to, I recommend renaming in the same folder.

Numerous options are available in the list boxes under File Naming. I normally use the date and subject as the filename with a 3- or 4-digit serial number. In Figure 1.13, all the images will be renamed to 0504_bodie_0123.DCR. Bodie is the subject, the images are from May 2004, and 0123 will be the sequential numbers created automatically. Batch rename shows an example of the filename.

Figure 1.13
Using Batch Rename gives a number of options for file naming. I usually use date_ subject_serialnumber.

> **Note:** To paraphrase the Wizard of Oz, pay no attention to that file extension! Batch rename will not convert your files to GIF or use .gif as the extension. It's just there as an example.

Bridge offers more options with Batch Rename, which is found under Tools > Batch Rename (as shown in Figure 1.14). Bridge includes the option to make a copy of the file rather than renaming and moving the original.

Using Metadata

Metadata is a fancy way of saying "extra information." All digital cameras store metadata, typically in what is known as EXIF format. EXIF, or Exchangeable Image File format, is a standard way of storing information about the camera and its settings, and it normally includes date and time, shutter speed, aperture, focal length, flash information, and other shooting data. Figure 1.15 shows what kind of information is found in a typical image file.

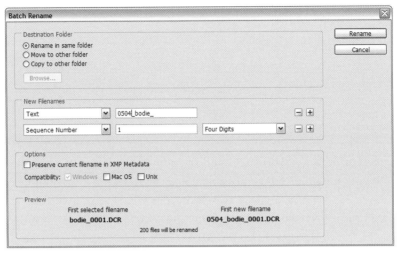

Figure 1.14 Batch Rename in Bridge offers more functionality than Photoshop Elements.

Figure 1.15
The information shown here is typical for most digital cameras and includes shooting information, date and time, file type, and file size.

In addition to the EXIF data recorded when the photo is taken, most cataloging programs support additional information to be included in the metadata. To help you find that image of the heron in a catalog of hundreds or thousands of photos, you can create keywords and assign them to images. Both Photoshop Elements and Photoshop support the addition of keywords to images. In both applications, keywords can be created and edited in the File Browser. The Windows version of Elements has an even easier way of assigning metadata by using Organizer's Tags feature, which I'll cover in the next few pages.

Defining Keywords

Coming up with a standard system of organizing your images is a critical part of using metadata. As your image collection grows, you'll appreciate having a list of standard keywords that you can call on to find the photo you are seeking.

I also recommend that you use enough categories and keywords to actually find what you're trying to locate. Spend some time up front thinking about the kinds of photographs you take and how you usually look for them. A nature photographer is likely to use a completely different set of categories and keywords than the sports photographer, but what the two will have in common is that each subject they shoot can be found by selecting a category and keyword to identify it.

For example, I have tagged some files with the following:

- Mountains (category)
- Cascades
- Eruption
- St. Helens
- Volcano
- Washington

Searching for any of these keywords will find the photo I'm after, but using multiple keywords will narrow down the list of possible images significantly. I have mountain images from all over. However, if a client calls and needs an image of a volcano in the Cascades, I can select those keywords to search on and reduce the number of possible images. Mt. Fuji and Moana Loa will be excluded from the resulting list because neither is in the Cascades.

> **Note:** Assign keywords every time you import images. You are much more likely to assign meaningful keywords at the time of import than you are later on when overwhelmed by hundreds or thousands of images.

Tags in Organizer

Creating tags in Organizer couldn't get much easier. Figure 1.16 shows the various tag creation dialogs, but you can also right-click a tag to create a new one.

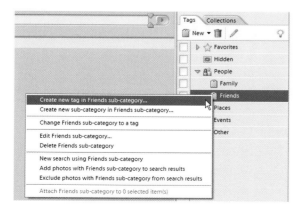

Figure 1.16

(top) Tags can be created by selecting New in the Tags panel. (bottom) You can also create them by right-clicking an existing tag.

Tags are organized in categories. Each category can contain tags or sub-categories or both. If you were to create a set of tags for bird images, you might have a structure similar to this:

- Birds - category
  - Raptors - sub-category
    - Eagle - tag
    - Hawk - tag
  - Wading - sub-category
    - GBH - tag
    - Egret - tag

The advantage to this type of tagging system becomes obvious when you start to use it. When you're ready to find bird images, you have multiple options that are only a click away. If you want to find all birds, click the checkbox next to the Birds category. Everything within that, in this case Eagle, Hawk, GBH (Great Blue Heron), and Egret will be displayed.

If you want only the Raptors, checking that tag will display only the Eagle and Hawk images. And, finally, checking Hawk will display only those images with the Hawk tag.

Keywords in File Browser and Bridge

Photoshop Elements File Browser and Bridge don't offer the same level of convenience that Organizer does, but assigning keywords is still easily done. The techniques described here apply to both Macintosh and Windows users of Bridge and Macintosh users of File Browser.

To create a keyword in either application, select the Keywords tab. Clicking on the folder icon ▭ will create a new Keyword Set that acts as a top-level grouping for similar keywords. The folded page icon ▤ will create a new keyword that will be placed in the current Keyword Set. If you wanted to create a new set of keywords, you would start by creating the Keyword Set and naming it. Using the earlier example of Birds, you would create a set for Raptors and another for Wading. With the Raptors set selected, create keywords for Eagle and Hawk.

You may have noticed that I created these sets a bit differently than the Organizer example. Bridge and File Browser don't allow nested sets, so creating one main set for birds with subsets isn't possible here.

To apply the keywords to one or more images, select them in the thumbnail view and click on each keyword you want to assign, as shown in Figure 1.17.

Figure 1.17

To apply keywords in File Browser (Macintosh only) and Bridge, select the images and check the keywords to assign.

File Browser and Bridge also include a dialog interface to create keywords and other metadata. Select one or more images in the Thumbnail panel and then select File > File Info. Figure 1.18 shows the dialog box displayed when multiple files are selected. To apply values to every selected image, check the box next to the field name. In this example, every selected image will have my name, web address, copyright information, and the displayed keywords added to them.

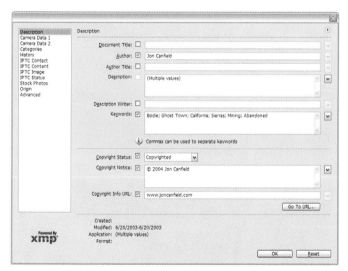

Figure 1.18 Using the File Info dialog is a quick and easy method of applying Metadata and Keywords to images in both File Browser and Bridge.

By clicking the arrow at the upper right of the dialog box, you can save the information as a template that can be applied to future images. This is especially useful for items that you want applied to every image, such as copyright information.

Rating and Flagging Images

Image ratings can be a boon when you are trying to select the best image in a group of very similar images. Organizer and Bridge offer rating systems that allow you to assign from zero to five stars to images. Bridge adds the ability to color code your images to help with the selection and editing process. For example, you could select all images of a particular color code to be printed or used in a slideshow.

File Browser does not support ratings. It has an option to flag files, but this should not be confused with ratings. Flagging is useful for making selections before batch renaming or bulk deleting; however, because an image is either flagged or not flagged, the ability to filter using this method is less useful for other operations.

 Note: You can fake the ratings support in File Browser by defining a Keyword Set named Rating and using 1–5 for the keywords in that set. Clumsy, but it'll do in a pinch.

Ratings are purely subjective and have no real meaning to others. Use them critically to help you find your best images. After all, if you give every image five stars, the ratings become useless for finding the best of the bunch.

Adobe Organizer

Organizer uses the Favorites tag set to apply ratings to images. To access the ratings tags, expand the Favorite set by clicking on the triangle next to the star in the Tags pane, as shown in Figure 1.19.

To apply ratings to photos you can either drag the star tag onto the photos, or you can drag the photos onto the tags, just like all the other tags. Unlike the other tags though, only one rating tag can be applied to each photo.

1. Start off by selecting the photo(s) you want to rate. To select multiple images, press the Ctrl key while clicking each image.

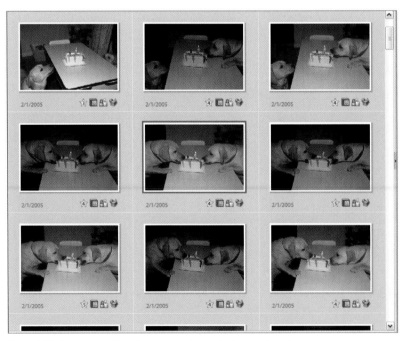

Figure 1.19 Organizer uses Favorites tags to assign one to five stars to an image.

2. Either drag the desired star tag onto the images or drag the selected images onto the desired star tag. After making your selections, you'll see a small star below each thumbnail you updated (Figure 1.20).

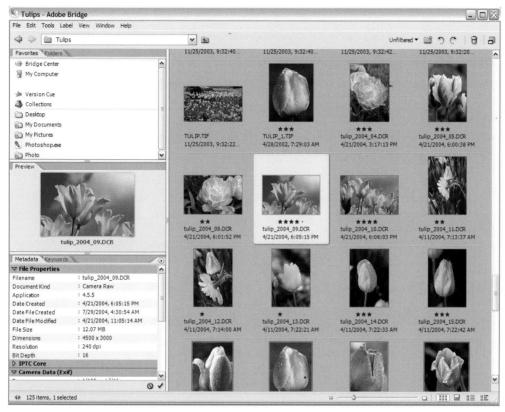

Figure 1.20 Organizer shows the ratings for each image just below its thumbnail. In this example, the icons show that each image has a Rating, and is assigned to a Collection and has People and Other Tags.

To change the rating of an image, simply repeat Steps 1 and 2. If you want to remove the rating completely, right-click on the star below the thumbnail and select Remove Stars tag.

Note: You can only remove rating stars from one image at a time.

Adobe Bridge

Adobe Bridge, part of Photoshop CS2, also has the ability to add star ratings of zero to five to images. To create ratings in Bridge, do the following.

1. Select the photo(s) you want to rate. To select multiple photos, press the Ctrl key (Windows) or Command key (Mac OS) while clicking each photo.

2. On any of the selected thumbnails, click on one of the five dots below the thumbnail and above the filename. The dots will update to show the number of stars assigned to the images, as shown in Figure 1.21.

3. Alternatively, you can select the Label menu and the number of stars to assign, or you can press the Ctrl/Cmd key plus the number of stars to assign. Pressing Ctrl+,/Cmd+, (comma) will decrease the rating by one star; Ctrl+./Cmd+. (period) will increase it by one.

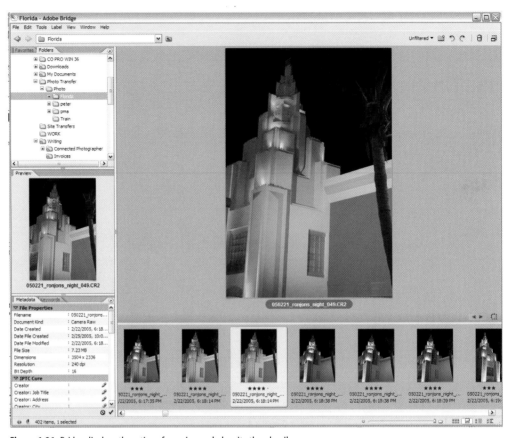

Figure 1.21 Bridge displays the ratings for an image below its thumbnail.

To remove ratings from one or more images, select them as described in Step 1 and either select Label > No Rating (Ctrl+0/Cmd+0) or click the symbol in front of the first star below the image thumbnail (Figure 1.22).

Figure 1.22
Clicking the symbol in front of any stars will turn off ratings for the selected images.

Selecting Images for Conversion

Wouldn't it be great if every image we took was perfect and worthy of printing or sharing? It would certainly save time and effort. After all, if all our shots were perfect, we'd probably take fewer photos. And we'd know up front that every photo we took was going to be converted from RAW to TIFF for touchup and other work.

Since every image isn't perfect, many serious photographers tend to have many variations of the same subject. Slight changes to composition, depth of field, and other creative aspects of an image are common and result in a large number of files to review.

Selecting by Keywords

If you've been diligent about assigning keywords, or tags, to your images as you add them to your collection, an easy way to select images for further processing is by keyword selection.

Both Bridge and File Browser have very similar search features, as seen in Figures 1.23 and 1.24.

Figure 1.23 Bridge Search is accessed by selecting Edit > Find.

Figure 1.24 File Browser Search is accessed by selecting File > Search.

Multiple keywords can be searched by clicking the plus (+) button; up to three keywords can be searched with File Browser and up to 13 with Bridge. With File Browser, multiple keywords can be searched only as an "AND" operation. For example, the search shown in Figure 1.25 will only find images that contain Luke *and* Clay as keywords.

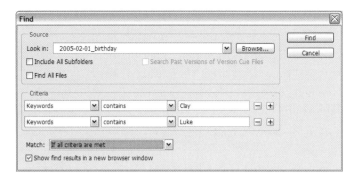

Figure 1.25

Multiple keywords can be used to narrow down the number of files found.

If Clay is removed from the search, then all images that contain Luke will be seen (Figure 1.26).

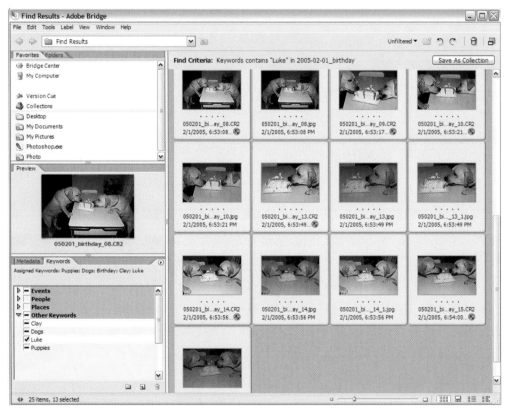

Figure 1.26 By removing Clay from the search, all images that have the keyword Luke are displayed even if other subjects are in the image.

Bridge has quite a bit more flexibility in its search settings. To match the results with the previous example in File Browser, click the Match dropdown list and select If All Criteria Are Met. To change the search to an "OR" operation, select If Any Criteria Are Met. This will find and display any images that have the keywords Luke *or* Clay.

Another difference between File Browser and Bridge search dialogs are the Criteria from which you can select. File Browser has an option to search by Flag, while Bridge includes options to search by Rating or Label among other options.

Organizer handles things a bit differently. Rather than using a Search dialog, you simply check the boxes next to the tags, or keywords, that you want to find. I love the simplicity of this method. Clicking one or more tags allows you to build a complex selection without much effort. Unfortunately, trying to get to the right tags in a group of many tags can be frustrating.

In the example shown in Figure 1.27, the tags selected for searching are shown with a binocular icon.

As with File Browser, multiple tag selections work as an AND. In this example, Organizer would find only those images that were tagged with Kathy, Ken, Erin, Bo, Rose, Clay, and Luke. It's not likely that many images would contain all of these tags so you can modify the search to perform as an OR by clicking the Close checkbox above the thumbnails as I've done here.

Figure 1.27 Searches in Organizer are done by selecting tags.

In addition to selecting directly from tags, a wealth of options that are useful for finding images is available in the Find menu (Figure 1.28). In particular, selecting by date range and History come in handy to only show images within a particular set of dates, or images that you have submitted or used previously.

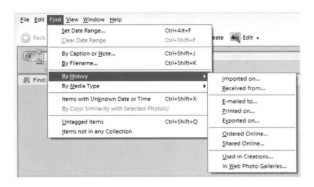

Figure 1.28 Additional selection options are available in the Find menu.

Selecting by Rating and Label

Users of Organizer, Bridge, and many other tools (such as iPhoto) can also select by rating. If you have a large group of similar images, it can be effective to make a selection based on keywords and then narrow down the results by using ratings. In Bridge, this can be done as part of the search by adding a Rating criteria. Figure 1.29 shows a search that will return all of the images with wading birds that are rated four stars or better.

Figure 1.29 You can build complex searches easily by using ratings along with keywords.

Alternatively, you can narrow down the selection after the search by selecting the rating or label from the Filter list at the top of the Bridge thumbnail view (Figure 1.30).

Figure 1.30

In Bridge you can select Ratings and Labels from the Filter list, or you can do so by typing a shortcut.

Rating selections in Organizer are done the same way as other tags. Clicking the box next to the Rating tag will select all images with that rating. To select more than one rating level, click each rating tag you want. For example, selecting the 4 Stars and 3 Stars tags will show all images that are rated at three or four.

In addition to ratings, Bridge adds labels to further help identify images. Figure 1.31 shows a Bridge window with rated and labels thumbnails. In this example, I've used yellow labels for all images of eruptions and blue labels for everything else to help quickly select types of images.

Figure 1.31 Bridge also includes labels as a way to further group images.

Summary

I've covered quite a bit of ground in this chapter. Although the information is directly about RAW images, establishing a good workflow is critical to the digital darkroom and will make your future image editing more productive, giving you time to work on the images rather than looking for them. Now then, let's get on to the good stuff: working with your RAW images!

Adobe Camera Raw

2

Photoshop Elements became a legitimate tool for serious photographers with version 3. Its ability to work with RAW images and its support for 16-bit files mean that you can now use it to do most of the editing tasks that previously required Photoshop. In this chapter, I'll introduce you to Adobe Camera Raw (ACR), the conversion tool included in Elements 3. I'll also call out differences between the Photoshop Elements and Photoshop versions of ACR. You'll be happy to know that for the majority of users, ACR and Elements can handle all the RAW processing tasks you might have.

Chapter Contents

Camera Raw versus Other Converters

With so many options available for RAW image conversion, why should you consider Adobe Camera Raw? After all, your camera probably came with conversion software. That software could be as basic as Nikon's PictureProject or Viewer, which offer basic correction to white balance and exposure, or as full-featured as Canon's Digital Photo Pro, which gives you full access to everything that you might want to do with a RAW file prior to conversion.

Note: I don't include the full-featured Nikon Capture in this list because it is a separate purchase—an error on Nikon's part, in my mind.

In my experience, camera companies are much better at designing cameras than they are at designing software—and when you use most of their tools, it shows. "Good user interface" and "performance" are not terms usually associated with the provided conversion tools.

There are also numerous other tools available to handle processing tasks—and some of them are quite good indeed, rivaling Adobe Camera Raw for functionality and quality. In particular, Capture One from Phase One (www.phaseone.com) and Bibble from Bibble Labs (www.bibblelabs.com) are both very powerful converters that operate on both Macintosh and Windows systems and provide the user with a wealth of RAW conversion options. These are all extra cost options though, and many may not be willing, or able, to justify them.

The one thing that none of these options provides is a tight integration with Photoshop or Photoshop Elements. Adobe has invested considerable time and effort into making ACR one of the premier converters available, and it shows. The advantages to ACR are apparent from the start if you are a Photoshop (Figure 2.1) or Elements user (Figure 2.2). The dialog and controls are laid out in a consistent and familiar way to keep the learning curve to a minimum.

Camera Raw also has another advantage that shouldn't be overlooked or underestimated: if you change camera brands at some point (and many of us do), there are no new programs to learn. If ACR supports the RAW files produced by your camera, it will look and work the same, regardless of camera type. As someone who has gone from one manufacturer to another, I find that I spend my time perfecting images and not learning new software; therefore, this converter "sameness" is both comforting and productive.

If you're just starting out with image editing and have chosen Photoshop Elements, or you work in an environment with both Elements and Photoshop, the RAW converter you've learned will still be there with the same interface and controls (along with a handful of new and useful advanced tools) if or when you move up to Photoshop.

Figure 2.1 The version of Adobe Camera Raw included with Photoshop CS2 offers more options than the Elements version, but both use the same conversion process.

Figure 2.2 Befitting the easier less-is-more approach that Elements takes, the version of ACR included here has fewer options (note the lack of tabs) but the same general layout.

Using the Preview Area

The Preview area of ACR is used for overall previews (kind of makes sense, doesn't it?) of all the editing operations you'll be performing on the RAW image prior to conversion. Because Photoshop Elements and Photoshop have different tools, I'll cover each of them separately. Figure 2.3 shows the preview area along with the controls available to help with image correction.

Figure 2.3 The Preview area of Photoshop CS2's version of Camera Raw will help you determine the best settings for the image prior to conversion, and it lets you crop and straighten an image.

In contrast, fewer controls are available in the Photoshop Elements version of Camera Raw, as seen in Figure 2.4. This version of Camera Raw is very similar to the one included with the earlier release of Photoshop CS, but it adds Auto settings.

Above the preview window, you'll find a toolbar of icons for basic tasks as shown in Figure 2.5.

Note: The Elements version of ACR includes the same Zoom, Hand, and White Balance tools as Photoshop CS2, but the Elements version does not include the Crop or Straighten tools. The Rotate buttons are still present, but they are not in the toolbar. In Elements, you'll find them at the lower right under the Preview area.

Figure 2.4 The Preview area for Photoshop Elements Camera Raw is laid out a bit differently than Photoshop CS2, and it has fewer options.

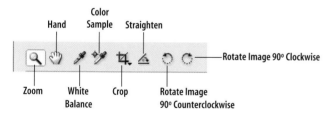

Figure 2.5 The toolbar in Camera Raw contains several basic image-editing tools.

Zoom and Hand Tools

The Zoom tool [magnifying glass icon] allows you to zoom in on a portion of the image in the preview area. You can zoom in one of two ways. A simple click will zoom in with the larger image centered on the point you clicked (Figure 2.6).

The Zoom tool works the same way as the one in Photoshop and Elements. Holding down the Alt/Option key while clicking will zoom out. (The pointer will change to a magnifying glass with a minus sign [icon].) The Zoom tool can be selected from the keyboard by pressing the Z key.

To have more control over how much you zoom in, you can click and drag a zoom area. The preview will zoom in to show you the area you selected, as shown in Figure 2.7.

Figure 2.6 Using the Zoom tool with a simple click will zoom the preview image centered on the click.

Figure 2.7 By dragging a selection with the Zoom tool, you can control how much image area you'll see in the preview window.

Note: As with almost everything in Photoshop, there's more than one way to zoom in. Just below the Preview area, you'll find a list box with preset sizes. Selecting one of these will magnify or reduce the image size. This is a good way to get back to a view that shows everything. You can also use the keyboard shortcuts listed in the Appendix to zoom in or out in the Preview area.

The Hand tool allows you to move your image around in the preview area. This can be useful when you are working on an image that is zoomed in. Rather than zooming back out, just click the Hand tool (or press **H** on the keyboard) and drag the image in the preview area to change what is seen. As a short cut, hold down the spacebar to activate the Hand tool without changing the selected tool.

Note: Zooming in on areas of the image is a good method for checking for critical sharpness prior to conversion.

Crop and Straighten Tools (Photoshop CS2 Only)

Photoshop CS2 introduced the Crop ⬜ and Straighten ⬜ tools to Camera Raw. Prior to this, and still the case in Photoshop Elements, cropping and straightening had to be done after the conversion process.

The ACR Crop tool works in the same manner as the Crop tool on the main Tools palette. Dragging out a selection in the Preview window will display a darkened mask around the selected area. The Crop tool also has an option to set specific dimensions for the crop, which are accessed by clicking and holding the mouse button on the Crop tool until the menu pops up. In addition to the preset options, you can create custom settings, which will then be displayed in the toolbar (Figure 2.8). For details on using custom Crop settings, see Chapter 6, "Advanced Conversion Options."

Figure 2.8

(left) The Crop tool can be set to crop to specific dimensions. (right) Custom settings are then available from the toolbar.

Once an image is cropped in Camera Raw (as seen in Figure 2.9) and then converted, the image will be opened at the selected size in Photoshop.

Figure 2.9 The selected area will be converted and opened in Photoshop at the size selected. In this example, the image will be 8×10 at 300 pixels per inch.

The Straighten tool is in reality a crop tool with a helpful line to straighten horizons. To use the Straighten tool, select it in the toolbar. Next, click at the starting point of a line that should be straight and drag across to the ending point, as shown in Figure 2.10. When you release the mouse button, a crop will be created with the angle you selected.

 Note: You can straighten a horizon with the Crop tool as well. Just move the mouse pointer to the masked area of the image, and it will change to a curved double arrow. Dragging up or down will rotate the crop selection.

Figure 2.10 The Straighten tool can help you quickly and accurately correct a horizon that is crooked.

Rotate Tools

Both the Photoshop Elements and Photoshop CS2 versions of Camera Raw include Rotate Image 90° Counterclockwise ↺ and Rotate Image 90° Clockwise ↻ tools. In Photoshop Elements, the tools are located below the Preview window. Photoshop CS2 moves these tools up to the toolbar with the other adjustment tools. Rotate is pretty obvious: clicking simply turns the image in the indicated direction. The Rotate tools also work by pressing **R** or **L** on the keyboard.

White Balance Tool

The White Balance tool ✎ can help you quickly correct color balance problems in a RAW image. The tool works by sampling the color under the pointer. When that color is selected by clicking the mouse button, it becomes neutral in tone. To help determine whether a color is close to neutral in tone, the R, G, and B (Figure 2.11) values are updated as the pointer is moved.

 Note: Neutral does not mean 18% gray. The White Balance tool sets neutral to be equal amounts of Red, Green, and Blue.

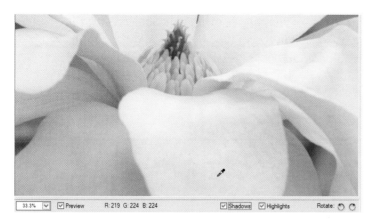

Figure 2.11
As you move the mouse pointer around the image area, the RGB values will change, showing you the relative amount of each color in that area of the image. Clicking the mouse with the White Balance tool will set all three color values to equal.

Note: Holding down the Alt/Option key will activate the Zoom Out tool and the Shift key will activate the White Balance tool when Zoom, Move, or White Balance are active. Releasing the key will return you to your regularly scheduled tool.

For more information on the White Balance tool and color temperature, see Chapter 3, "RAW Conversion."

Color Sampler Tool (Photoshop CS2 Only)

The Color Sampler tool lets you take up to nine measurements. The only real value I can see in the Color Sampler is when you are using the Calibrate options, or identifying a critical area for highlight and shadow detail adjustment. I'll cover this option in Chapter 6.

Workflow Settings

The final area of the Preview window to look at is the Workflow Settings. As with the Toolbar options, Photoshop has more options here (Figure 2.12) than in the version of Camera Raw included with Elements.

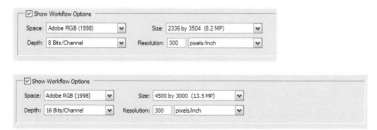

Figure 2.12 (top) The Photoshop CS2 Workflow Settings area, located below the Preview window, contains options for setting the bit depth, color space, resolution, and image size. (bottom) The Elements version of Camera Raw has fewer options than its big brother. You'll be able to set the bit depth, preview size, and rotation, as well as highlight and shadow warnings.

Photoshop has full color management support, and it lets you select from four different color spaces when converting a RAW file. Of the four, Adobe RGB (1998) is the most commonly used color space, and it is an appropriate choice for general image editing. ProPhoto RGB is a bit larger color space than Adobe RGB (1998), and it is preferred by many pro shooters for the slightly wider color range possible. sRGB IEC61966-1 is designed for screen display, such as web browsers or digital slideshows. Unless you know in advance that your image conversion is only going to be used for screen display, Adobe RGB (1998) or ProPhoto RGB will be the best choices.

Note: Color management is the term given to the process of making sure that your image's color is consistent from one device (such as the monitor) to another (such as your printer). Each of these devices uses profiles to understand how to handle color. This is a topic unto itself and goes beyond the scope of this book. I highly recommend *Color Confidence* by Tim Grey (Sybex, 2004) for more in-depth information on color management.

Shadows and Highlights Clipping

Here's some advice: make life easier for yourself and turn on Shadows and Highlights clipping by checking the boxes. When combined with the histogram, this is far and away the best tool in Adobe Camera Raw to monitor exposure information in your images. Without these two options enabled, you're just guessing at how much detail you can pull from your photo.

As an example, I'll start with the image shown in Figure 2.13. I know that this image has room for improvement in the shadows and highlights because the histogram shows the image data ending before it reaches either end of the histogram.

Note: Clipping is the loss of image data, where highlights are completely white and shadows completely black. Generally, this is a bad thing.

To start with, I'll add more detail in the Shadows through the Shadows slider. To increase shadow detail, move the slider to the right. As soon as I pass the maximum for the image, the preview shows information that is beyond the useable range in bright blue (Figure 2.14). At this point, back off the shadow level until the blue is gone.

Repeating the process for the highlights, I adjust the Exposure slider until I see bright red (Figure 2.15). Again, back off the Exposure level until the red is gone.

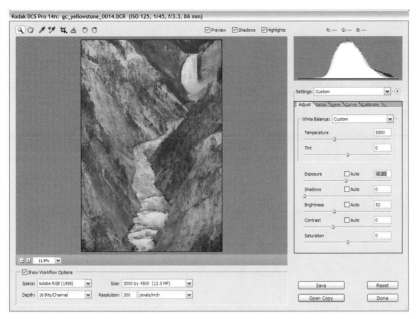

Figure 2.13 This image needs more shadow detail. By turning on the Shadows clipping warning, I can see when I've gone as far as possible.

Figure 2.14 The bright blue spots (at bottom right and along the riverbank) indicate areas that have lost all detail and will display as pure black.

Figure 2.15 Clipped highlights are displayed in bright red when the Highlights checkbox is selected.

Not every image needs to have the maximum shadow and highlight detail, though. Some images, such as low contrast images like a foggy landscape , would not benefit from both of these adjustments. I'll cover these types of images later, but for now it's good to know how to verify that your image isn't going beyond the limits of what you can display or print.

Setting Bit Depth

One of the biggest advantages of shooting in RAW is the additional bit depth available in your image. RAW captures are typically 10 to 14 bits per color channel. The key to taking advantage of this extra color information is the Bit Depth setting in Camera Raw. The Depth setting offers two choices: 8 Bits/Channel and 16 Bits/Channel. Eight-bit images contain a maximum of 256 values per color. Sixteen-bit images, on the other hand, provide 32,768 possible values per color. This extra bit depth is one of the reasons to shoot RAW over JPEG. The extra values greatly reduce the chances of banding, or abrupt changes in tone, and allow more aggressive edits to correct your images. When saving a file at 8 Bits/Channel, color information is discarded, reducing both image quality and the ability to make editing changes without risk of significant image degradation. Because you shoot RAW for maximum image quality, I recommend using the 16 Bits/Channel setting to retain all the color information in your original file.

 Note: If you know that a file will only be used on the Web, or in a slideshow, 8 Bits/Channel might seem like a logical choice. I recommend converting at 16 Bits/Channel and doing all image edits before converting to 8-bit as the final step.

Many of the editing tasks that you'll perform after converting from RAW to TIFF are considered *destructive* edits, meaning that the image data is changed and cannot be recovered. When working with 8 bits of data per color, these changes are seen with less aggressive edits, giving you less latitude to make corrections to your images.

Bit depth is the one case where I would suggest that you always use the highest setting or level possible. If you are going to take the time and effort to shoot in RAW for maximum quality, why would you immediately throw out color information before you even get started?

Of course, high bit-depth files have their unique drawbacks. Chief among these is file size. A 16-bit TIFF file is going to be roughly twice the size of its 8-bit counterpart. Consider a typical RAW file from the Canon 1D Mark II. As a RAW file, it uses about 8MB of disk space. Opening that file as an 8-bit TIFF increases the size to 23.4MB. That same file converted to a 16-bit TIFF uses 46.8MB of disk space.

Understanding the Histogram

The histogram is your key to understanding where tonal values are in the image. A histogram represents the range of tone from pure black on the left to pure white on the right. The height of the columns in the histogram indicates how many pixels of that tone are present in the image. In the histogram shown in Figure 2.16, very few pixels in the image are black or white, and the bulk of the pixels are in the upper midtones, which are represented by the taller bars in the histogram.

Ideally, your images will have all the data between these two end points, whether the data is distributed evenly from dark to light or is exposed as far to one end as possible without losing, or clipping, information. The image in Figure 2.16 is an example of a properly exposed photo. All of the image data lies between the black end point and white end point of the histogram.

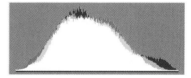

Figure 2.16 This image is properly exposed. All image data is contained within the histogram, which shows that no information is being lost or "clipped" at either end of the scale.

If you view your image and see a histogram similar to the ones in Figure 2.17, either the exposure was wrong or the dynamic range of the image was wider than the camera was able to capture. Image information that is beyond the range the camera can capture will be displayed as pure black or pure white.

Figure 2.17 (left) This histogram is from an image that is underexposed. Most of the data in this image is in the left side of the histogram. Every pixel at the left edge of the histogram will be displayed as pure black. (right) The histogram for an overexposed image. In this case, every pixel at the right edge of the histogram will be displayed as pure white without any detail.

Figure 2.18 When all of the image information is bunched together in the histogram, the image will look flat with no true shadow or highlight detail. This is easy to correct with the adjustment sliders.

Another problematic area for your image can appear when all of the data in the histogram is bunched together with empty space between the edges of the histogram and the start of your image information, as shown in Figure 2.18. This type of histogram can indicate a flat, low contrast image that is lacking true shadows and highlights. Luckily, this is also the easiest problem to correct. All of the image information is there and usable. It's up to you to bring out that detail through adjustments to exposure, shadows, highlights, and contrast.

The histogram is one of the most valuable tools at your disposal when you are making adjustments to the image. By monitoring the effect of changes to exposure, shadows, highlights, and contrast, you can maximize the tonal range of your image while preventing detail from being lost through adjustments that are too aggressive. In the next section, I'll show you how to use both the histogram and the Shadows and Highlights warnings to get the most from your RAW file prior to conversion.

The histogram displays red, green, and blue values individually. In addition to these colors, you'll see cyan, magenta, yellow, and white displayed in the histogram (Figure 2.19). These colors show where there is overlap between the different color channels:

- **Cyan** indicates pixels where both blue and green are present.
- **Magenta** represents the overlap between red and blue.
- **Yellow** shows pixels that contain both red and green.
- **White** indicates pixels that have data from all three color channels.

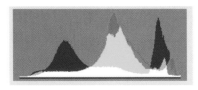

Figure 2.19

The Histogram display shows each color channel and the number of pixels that contain data for multiple color channels.

Understanding the Adjustment Sliders and Auto Controls

Photoshop Elements 3 and Photoshop CS2 added a new feature to Camera Raw that promises to save you time with image adjustments. The Exposure, Shadows, Highlights, and Contrast sliders all have an Auto checkbox, as shown in Figure 2.20. Auto for these controls works similarly to the Auto Levels, Contrast, and Color settings you may be used to from the Image > Adjustments menu in Photoshop CS and the Enhance menu in Photoshop Elements. The Auto checkbox is a nifty little tool; however, it isn't a cure all.

Figure 2.20

Adobe Camera Raw now includes Auto checkboxes for common image corrections. Like the Auto Levels, Contrast, and Color settings from Photoshop and Photoshop Elements, they aren't the perfect choices for every image. However, they can serve as good starting points for your corrections.

As with any Auto feature, it's important to understand how the settings work and when they should or shouldn't be used. Chapter 3 goes into detail on using each of these controls to fine-tune your image. The examples here show how the Auto settings can work for you or against you.

The Auto settings can be useful starting points for your image corrections, though. Figure 2.21 is an admittedly extreme example of what the Auto checkboxes can do for you. This shot of the New York area, which was taken from an airliner, goes from almost black to a well-exposed image by using only the Auto settings.

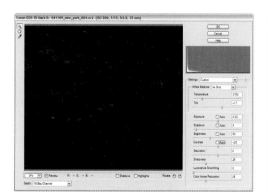
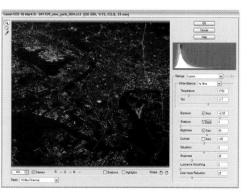

Figure 2.21 (left) Here you see New York from the air. With Auto settings disabled, the image is primarily black with a few dots of light. (right) With Auto checked for each of the controls, the same image shows the detail and scene as I remember it.

In contrast to the New York photo, the image from Bodie, CA (a ghost town in the Sierra Nevada mountains) shown in Figure 2.22, is an example of when the Auto settings are too aggressive. With the Highlights and Shadows checkboxes enabled, it's clear that the Auto settings added too much exposure and shadow to the image, resulting in lost data. Making these adjustments manually, I was able to retain significant detail that would have been lost at both ends of the tonal range if I had converted with the Auto settings.

Unless you save custom defaults for Camera Raw settings, turning off Auto will use the in-camera settings that were in effect when the image was captured.

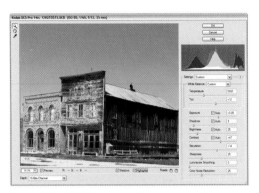

Figure 2.22 (left) This image is going to lose significant amounts of shadow and highlight detail if the Auto settings are used. (right) By setting these controls manually, I am able to retain detail what would have been otherwise lost.

Note: You can't hurt the image at this point by playing with the adjustment settings. Try the Auto settings on your image to see if they work. You might need only a slight adjustment.

Exposure

The Exposure slider allows you to make adjustments of up to four stops over or under to your RAW image. Using the Exposure slider is similar to setting exposure compensation in the camera when you capture an image. Unlike compensation set in camera though, modifying the exposure in Camera Raw will not recover information that is not there. In other words, if you've over or under exposed the image to the point where no information other than black or white is recorded, the Exposure slider isn't going to magically create that data for you. Adjustments to the Exposure slider can help make shadow areas less dense and highlights less bright, which will allow subtle detail that *was* hiding in those areas to be more obvious.

The Auto setting for Exposure works very similarly to the Auto Levels command in Photoshop and Photoshop Elements. It works by analyzing the image data and making adjustments to maximize the amount of tonal range in your image.

Note: Maximizing the tonal range is normally a good thing, but it is not appropriate for all images. High key images, for example, would have the majority of their tonal range at the highlight side of the histogram. Spreading the tonal range out across the entire possible range would take away from the effect.

The Exposure slider determines the brightness of the entire image, setting the brightest value the image will contain. If you are familiar with the Levels control, Exposure works the way the right slider in the Levels dialog does (Figure 2.23). The far left slider adjusts the black, or shadow point, the center slider adjusts the overall brightness of the image, and the right hand slider adjusts the highlight, or white point, of the image.

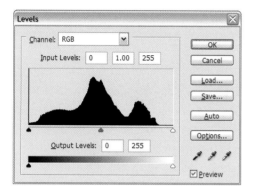

Figure 2.23

The Exposure, Shadows, and Brightness sliders work the same way the Input Level controls in Photoshop and Photoshop Elements work. The Exposure control is the same as the right slider, Shadows the left slider, and Brightness the center slider.

The best way to monitor your adjustments with the Exposure slider is to use the Alt/Option key while making adjustments Figure 2.24 shows what the preview display looks like when using this method. The colored pixels show which color channel is clipping. White pixels indicate all color channels are being clipped and will result in pure white. The Alt/Opt key method is much more detailed than the simple shadow and highlight clipping checkboxes, especially for exposure and shadow adjustments, because it shows each color channel as the image is adjusted.

Figure 2.24 Pressing the Alt/Opt key while adjusting the Exposure slider shows each color channel as it becomes clipped. White indicates all three colors are clipped and will be displayed as pure white in the converted image.

Shadows

The Shadows slider controls the black point in your image. The Shadows control is equivalent to the black point, or left slider in the Levels command. The Shadows slider has a range of 0 to 100, but typically you'll use values of 25 or less. The default setting for Shadows is 5 when Auto is unchecked. As with Exposure, the best way to monitor your adjustments with the Shadows slider is to use the Alt/Option key while making adjustments (Figure 2.25). The colored pixels show which color channel is clipping. White pixels indicate all color channels are being clipped and will result in pure black.

Brightness

The Brightness slider works to set the overall brightness of your image by moving the distribution of the pixels to the left or right without affecting the shadow or highlights. Like the Exposure and Shadows sliders, the Brightness slider also has an equivalent in the Levels command. Brightness works in the same manner as the center slider. To brighten the overall tone of an image, move the slider to the right. The slider has a range of 0 to 150 and defaults to 50 when Auto is unchecked.

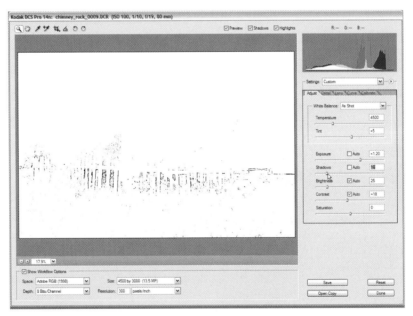

Figure 2.25 By holding down the Alt/Option key while adjusting the Shadows slider, you can easily see when detail is beginning to clip, or go out of range.

When using the Brightness slider, you'll need to keep an eye on the histogram to see where the color values are going to ensure that you don't begin clipping colors.

Contrast

The Contrast slider can add depth to your image and really make it come to life by adjusting the midtones. With a range of –50 to 100, the default setting is 25 when Auto is unchecked. Settings higher than 25 will add more contrast by darkening the values below the midtone and lightening those above the midtone. Reducing the setting below

25 will reduce contrast in the image by lightening the values below the midtone and darkening the values above it.

Contrast adjustments should be made after correcting Exposure, Shadows, and Brightness since these controls have more impact on the overall appearance of the image.

Fine Tuning

Saturation, Sharpness, Luminance Smoothing, and Color Noise Reduction are the final four controls that both Photoshop Elements and Photoshop CS2 versions of Camera Raw have in common. Photoshop Elements users will find all four of these sliders displayed below Contrast. Photoshop CS2 users will see the Saturation slider on this tab, while the others are found on the Details tab (Figure 2.26).

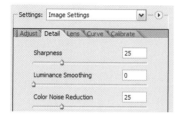

Figure 2.26

The Details tab in the Photoshop CS2 version of Camera Raw contains the Sharpness, Luminance Smoothing, and Color Noise Reduction sliders.

Saturation

Saturation defaults to 0, which is no change, and it is frequently best to leave it there. Possible values range from –100 to 100, or no saturation (black and white) to double the saturation. This is one of the few options that I prefer to wait until post processing to do. Because the amount of saturation needed will change depending on the intended use of the image, I feel that it is best done after conversion. I will often use different saturation settings for prints than I will for web or screen use.

> **Note:** You can make a quick conversion to grayscale by setting the Saturation slider to –100. You won't have the same level of control that you would have by using the Channel Mixer, but it is possible to create a good black-and-white image during conversion by using this method. After setting Saturation to the far left, adjustments to Contrast, Exposure, Shadows, and Brightness can yield good results that would otherwise take several steps in Photoshop CS2 or Photoshop Elements. I'll cover this technique in depth in Chapter 4, "Beyond the Basics."

Sharpness

Every digital image needs sharpening. That may sound like a bold statement, but it's true—especially for cameras that use an antialiasing filter (which most do) to reduce moiré in the photo. This antialiasing filter softens the image which needs to be corrected after exposure. When you shoot JPEG, the converter in your camera applies sharpening to the image automatically but this isn't true of RAW images. Camera Raw includes a Sharpness slider, so it would seem logical to use this to sharpen your image, right? Wrong! The problem with sharpening in Camera Raw is that you have very little control over how the sharpening is applied. It's also best to apply sharpening as one of the last steps in image processing because you'll have different needs depending on your output size and type. The sharpening you apply to a web image will almost certainly not be the same as you would apply to the same image for printing.

The Sharpness slider is a handy tool, though, for use while previewing your RAW adjustments because it will give you an approximation of how the image will appear when sharpened. In Photoshop CS2, to make sure that only the preview is sharpened and not the converted file, you can set the default in Camera Raw Preferences to Preview only. Click the triangle next to the Settings list, and select Preferences. In the Camera Raw Preferences dialog, select Preview Images Only from the Apply Sharpening To list.

If you use Camera Raw in Photoshop Elements, the Preferences option is not available. The safest method to avoid accidentally sharpening your image during conversion is to set the Sharpness slider to 0 and then save your settings as the new default. To do so, just click the triangle next to the Settings list and choose Set Camera Default. For detailed information on setting and using custom defaults, see Chapter 6.

Luminance Smoothing

The Luminance Smoothing slider controls the noise in the image that appears similar to film grain. This type of noise is usually apparent in digital images with dense shadow areas and those shot at higher ISO settings. Any adjustment to reduce this type of noise will soften the image, so it's best to critically examine the image during adjustment. I suggest zooming in to at least 100 percent and higher if needed. I often zoom in to 300 percent or more. on the area that you are concerned about and using the keyboard to make adjustments to Luminance Smoothing. The Up and Down arrow keys will make a one-step change with each key press.

Color Noise Reduction

Unlike the noise controlled with the Luminance Smoothing slider, Color Noise Reduction works on those irritating green and magenta toned spots that show up predominately in the shadow areas of your images, as appears in in Figure 2.27.

And, as with the Luminance Smoothing slider, it's critical to make minor adjustments while viewing the image at 100 percent or larger. Color Noise Reduction will also soften the image but not nearly as much as the Luminance Smoothing slider. It's up to you to decide whether the resulting softness is objectionable or not.

Note: Photoshop CS2 has a new Noise Reduction filter found under Filters > Noise > Reduce Noise. This filter offers much better control over the noise reduction process by allowing you to work on each color channel separately. For specific information on using the Reduce Noise filter, I recommend *Photoshop CS2 Workflow* by Tim Grey (Sybex, 2005).

Figure 2.27 Color noise is typically seen as green and magenta spots in the shadow areas of your image. It's more likely to occur with high ISO or long exposures.

> **Note:** Photoshop Elements also has the Reduce Noise filter, but it does not include the advanced features that are included with CS2.

Other Camera Raw Controls

Photoshop CS2 users will find additional controls in Camera Raw available to adjust chromatic aberration, lens vignetting, curves adjustment, and camera calibration. I'll cover all of these controls in Chapter 6, "Advanced Conversion Options."

Summary

Adobe Camera Raw has many options to help you convert your RAW images. Whether you use the version of Camera Raw in Photoshop Elements 3 or the more advanced version included with Photoshop CS2, with a little effort and practice you'll be able to get the maximum detail your camera is capable of delivering.

RAW Conversion

In Chapter 2, "Adobe Camera Raw," I walked through the Adobe Camera Raw converter and its options. In this chapter, I'll expand on how to use those controls by using numerous examples to give you a better understanding of how the controls respond. Mastery of these controls will give you the best possible image after conversion and minimize the amount of post processing work you'll need to do.

3

Chapter Contents

Setting White Balance

Unlike film, which is intended for specific lighting such as daylight or tungsten, digital media can be used in any light source by selecting the proper white balance, or color temperature, of the light used. Getting an accurate white balance can be a challenge, though, when shooting under different conditions.

The human eye does a great job of compensating for different lighting conditions. Regardless of what the light source is—incandescent, fluorescent, daylight, or firelight—we automatically adjust to see white as white.

Cameras, on the other hand, are very literal. They see exactly what shade of white is in the scene based on the lighting used. For incandescent or firelight situations, white is going to be seen with an orange or red tone. Fluorescent lighting will give that same white a greenish tint. This is because each of these light sources outputs a different color temperature.

One advantage to shooting in digital is that color temperature can be adjusted for each shot if needed. With film, color compensation filters or lighting changes are required to change the way it responds to light since the entire roll of film will react to light in the same way. Film is typically balanced for daylight or tungsten lighting. Using daylight-balanced film under tungsten lighting, such as a common light bulb, will result in photos with a strong orange or amber tone to them. To compensate using traditional methods, you can use an 80A (blue) filter when shooting in these conditions; tungsten film in daylight can be corrected with the 85A (amber) filter. Fluorescent lighting, thanks to its variety of color temperatures, can be corrected with an FL-D or FL-B (magenta or amber) filter. All of this makes a digital camera's ability to set color temperature for individual situations without dealing with filters or film types very attractive. The adjustment to color temperature is referred to as *setting the white balance.*

All digital cameras offer automatic white balance. Most offer several different preset white balance settings as well, such as Cloudy, Tungsten, Fluorescent, Daylight, and Flash. Some of the more pro-oriented cameras will allow you to set the white balance to a specific temperature setting.

Which Adjustment First?

I usually prefer to make white balance adjustments before using any of the other adjustment controls in Camera Raw. The one exception to this is when the exposure is way off. This is a good general rule to follow.

White balance and exposure will be the first two adjustments made to an image—correct the one that is furthest from accurate first. Shadows, brightness, and contrast will follow these adjustments. Again, if brightness or contrast is way off, make adjustments to those settings first and then adjust the shadows.

As you make adjustments, you will likely find yourself going back to fine-tune the other sliders. RAW image conversion is often an iterative process with each slider affecting the other.

In general, the Auto setting works well, especially when shooting RAW. Because the actual white balance isn't being applied to the RAW image, it's easy to change this after the fact in Adobe Camera Raw.

Using White Balance Presets

Adobe Camera Raw includes all of the common white balance presets. If you know that a particular image was shot under one of these lighting conditions, correction can be as simple as making a selection from the list. I find that these presets do a good job of getting me close to the white balance I want, but they seldom hit exactly on the right color.

The presets, as seen in Figure 3.1, include all of the common lighting conditions as well as three additional choices:

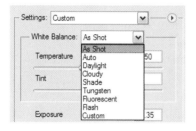

Figure 3.1

The list of preset white balance options in Adobe Camera Raw serves as a good starting point for making adjustments to your images.

- **As Shot** will use the setting from your camera if Camera Raw can read it. This is most useful if you've set a custom white balance in the camera, but many cameras do a good job with Auto White Balance and you may find that this setting works well for most of your images.

- **Auto** will attempt to correct the color balance to what Camera Raw thinks is correct. Camera Raw analyzes the image and makes a best guess at the correct white balance. Auto in Camera Raw is not the same as using the Auto setting in your camera. To use the camera's Auto, select As Shot.

- **Custom** will automatically be used whenever any adjustment is made to the Temperature or Tint sliders.

Figure 3.2 shows the same image using different white balance presets for an outdoor image. Any one of them could be correct depending on the light and look you want to convey, but each is very different from the other.

Which is correct? I know from the shooting conditions that the Daylight setting should give me the closest to the "correct" result, but otherwise I would have a hard time deciding which was technically *accurate*. Although Daylight is the closest setting to what I want, it isn't exactly what I'm looking for. By using the Temperature and Tint controls, you can adjust the white balance to the preferred setting for that image. Remember that photography is a creative process, and accurate is not always what you want to convey with your image.

Daylight   Cloudy   Shade

Figure 3.2 This series of images (all conversions of the same shot) shows how different white balance settings can be between Daylight, Cloudy, and Shade—all possible options for this particular image. The first example is with the Daylight setting of 5500. The Cloudy preset, with a setting of 6500, has a much warmer tone. The Shade preset, at 7500, is warmer yet; this one is obviously off to me, with much more yellow than I want.

Using the Temperature and Tint Controls

ACR offers multiple ways to select a color balance for your image. The most obvious of these are the White Balance dropdown list and the Temperature slider. The dropdown list is a great way to set gross white balance adjustments. By gross, I mean major changes such as when the image was captured with a Daylight white balance but the camera should have been set to Tungsten.

The Temperature slider can be used to move to a particular color temperature using the Kelvin scale. Kelvin uses a very wide range of temperatures, with midday sunlight typically around 5,500. Table 3.1 provides a more complete list of average temperatures.

▶ **Table 3.1** Approximate Kelvin Values for Common Lighting

Type of Lighting	Typical Temperature
Candlelight	1,900
Sunrise/sunset	2,000
Incandescent (tungsten)	2,800–3,200
Fluorescent (warm)	3,000
Halogen	3,000
Photofloods	3,200
Fluorescent (cool white)	3,800
Sunlight (morning/evening)	4,300
Sunlight (midday)/flash	5,500
Cloudy	6,500
Shade	7,500
Blue sky	12,000+

One technique that I find useful is to select a preset white balance from the list, such as Daylight, and then adjust the Temperature slider to give the image a warmer or cooler look.

For those times that you need absolute control over the white balance, or when you want to set a neutral point for your image but not remove a desired color cast, the White Balance tool can make the job a little easier.

Why would you want to leave a color cast in the image? Ask any nature photographer and you'll probably get the same answer: golden light at morning or evening. There are times when we strive for a particular feel to our images; Figure 3.3 is an example of this golden light. Without it, the image is a technically nice image, but lacks the feeling of the original scene.

Figure 3.3 (left) This image was adjusted for color temperature to be neutral in tone. While it's a very nice image, it has none of the warmth and atmosphere of the original image. (right) Same image, but with the correct color temperature. The rich golden light adds to the impact of the image. (Courtesy Art Morris, www.birdsasart.com)

Note: You can use the keyboard to adjust Temperature and Tint. The up and down arrows will adjust temperature by 50 and tint by 1. Adding Shift adjusts by 500 and 10 respectively.

You can fine-tune the color balance with the Temperature and Tint sliders. The Temperature slider displays the current color temperature in Kelvin, with lower numbers having more yellow and higher numbers having more blue. The control ranges from 2,000, which is very yellow, to 50,000, or very blue. It would be unusual to have an image that comes anywhere near the upper end of the scale, but the lower end is about the same as a dim candle.

Note: Wait a second! If cooler temperatures are higher numbers, why do you raise the Temperature setting to warm up an image? Good question and I'm glad you asked! Adjustments to the Temperature slider are actually compensating for the color temperature of the image. So if you move the slider to the left, you are adding blue to correct for the existing yellow light.

The Tint slider is used to adjust the magenta and green tones in the image. Moving the slider to the left, or toward the negative numbers, increases the amount of green while positive adjustments to the right increases the magenta in your image. The Tint slider has a range of –150, or very green, to +150, or very magenta. Most of your image edits, other than creative toning, won't be that extreme though—I seldom make a Tint adjustment of more than 20 to an image.

Starting with the same image used in the earlier example, Figure 3.4 shows the final image with the white balance fine-tuned. To reach the exact setting I was looking for, I chose the Daylight setting from the preset White Balance list; it was close but still a bit too warm. By moving the Temperature slider down to 4650, the white balance was corrected.

The Temperature and Tint sliders have an obvious use, but they can also be used for creative techniques such as toning images to emulate alternative processing, which I'll show you in Chapter 4, "Beyond the Basics."

Figure 3.4 I started with the Daylight setting, which was closest to "correct," and then I adjusted the Temperature slider until I ended up with this exposure, which has the color balance I remember from the scene. The final setting for the image was 4650.

Using the Exposure Control

The Exposure slider works like the exposure compensation setting on your camera. The numbers shown are equivalent to f-stops, with higher numbers adding more light to the scene and negative numbers subtracting light. The slider has a range of four stops in either direction, which gives you a great deal of control over the image after the capture. Large changes (over one full stop of additional exposure) are likely to introduce noise into the image that will need to be dealt with, so don't depend on Camera Raw to rescue every poorly exposed image you throw at it. If you've used the Levels command in Photoshop Elements or Photoshop, the Exposure control is similar in function to the far right, or white point, slider. The Exposure control in Camera Raw is much more powerful than a simple white point adjustment in the Levels command though, as you'll see here.

> **Note:** It's very seldom that you will make only a single adjustment in Camera Raw. Adjustments to exposure typically lead to adjustments in the other controls as well. The following examples are typical of the steps involved in correcting exposure.

I spend more time explaining exposure than any of the other topics in this chapter because exposure is critical to the quality of your converted image and it is the most powerful control in Adobe Camera Raw, allowing you to perform miracles or digital murder on your images.

Correcting Underexposure

In the typical image, you'll be adjusting the exposure to bring the white point of the image to the far right of the histogram. Underexposed images, such as the one in Figure 3.5, will need to have exposure added by moving the slider to the right. Although this particular image is an extreme example of underexposure, it does demonstrate what can be done by using RAW.

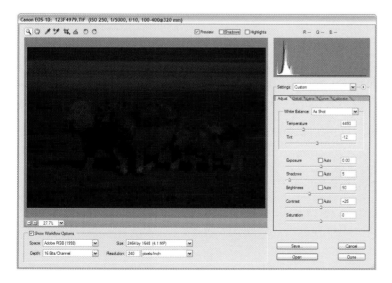

Figure 3.5 The original RAW image is severely underexposed. Had this been a JPEG file, the amount of detail recoverable would have made this image unusable. (Image courtesy of Art Morris, www .birdsasart.com)

As you can see, the histogram is compressed well to the left, or shadow side. To begin the correction, you'll drag the Exposure slider to the right. For this particular image, even a full four stops doesn't begin to clip the highlights, but the adjustments made a huge difference in the amount of detail available, as you can see from Figure 3.6.

Figure 3.6 After the Exposure control is adjusted, the image displays detail across the histogram.

Further adjustments to the other sliders in Camera Raw fine-tune the image for shadow and contrast. Adjustments to both the Temperature and Tint controls correct the color cast and white balance problems in the original image, as seen in Figure 3.7.

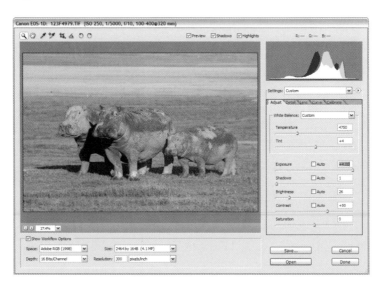

Figure 3.7 Additional adjustments made to Shadows, Brightness, Contrast, and White Balance have corrected the image further. Note that the histogram is more evenly distributed from shadow to highlight. Because of the amount of underexposure, it will be impossible to completely eliminate the loss of data on the shadow side of the histogram. I've made the best of the situation with these settings.

The final image, shown in Figure 3.8, has become very usable because of the latitude offered by the RAW format. With this much adjustment to the exposure, you can plan on having issues with noise. In this particular image the noise is noticeable but not objectionable. Other subjects, especially those where high levels of detail are visible, won't handle this much adjustment.

Figure 3.8 Shooting in RAW saved this image from the trashcan. No other format would have allowed such drastic editing.

> **Note:** Don't forget the Alt/Option key and slider adjustment combo that changes the preview display to help you determine problems when making exposure adjustments. Holding the key down while dragging the Shadows slider will turn the preview area into a clipping display.

Correcting Overexposure

Camera Raw's ability to correct an overexposure is excellent. Of course, that doesn't mean you can shoot without worrying about your exposure, but the RAW format does offer more latitude when making image corrections than other formats will. Unlike conventional tools, such as the Levels command, Camera Raw can recover highlight detail with a much greater amount of control. In fact, if there is still image data in even one color channel, Camera Raw can recover that detail. Of course, the more color channels that contain data, the better the recovery will be—but seeing how much can be gained from even one channel is pretty impressive. Figure 3.9 shows an image that is overexposed in the clouds. Notice that the histogram shows a spike on the right, or highlight side, and mostly in the blue channel.

I start off by moving the Exposure slider to the left, taking away light from the image. At –0.60, the highlights are no longer clipped. I can verify this by holding down the Alt/Option key while dragging the Exposure slider, which shows that no data is being clipped. Figure 3.10 shows the image after adjusting the exposure.

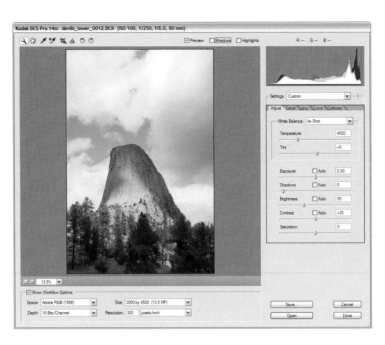

Figure 3.9 This image is over-exposed and has lost detail in the clouds. To correct this, the Exposure slider needs to be moved to the left.

As with the underexposed image in the previous example, adjustments are made to the Shadow, Brightness, Contrast, and Temperature sliders to finish the correction. The final image, shown in Figure 3.11, is significantly better in both tonal range and detail.

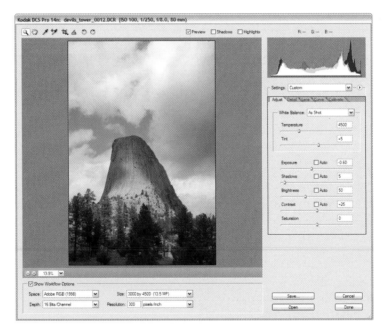

Figure 3.10 After lowering the exposure by almost $^2/_3$ of a stop, the highlights have moved within range and more detail is visible in the clouds.

The final image (shown in Figure 3.12) is much better than the original RAW file. Although this example isn't as extreme as the underexposed image, I would not have been able to recover the highlight detail in the clouds if it had been a JPEG file.

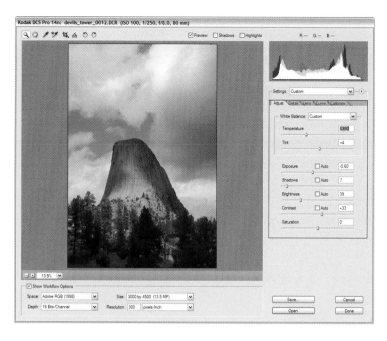

Figure 3.11 The final image settings are made to correct shadow and contrast along with color balance. The histogram is now much more evenly distributed.

Figure 3.12
The final image is corrected. Notice the additional detail in the highlights, as well as the stronger shadow areas.

The next example shows how well Camera Raw can recover detail in what looks like a hopelessly overexposed image. Figure 3.13 shows the starting image, a leaf in snow. I shot this without noticing that the camera was still set to manual exposure. The first lesson to be learned here is that 1/60 second at f5.6 isn't the right exposure for bright sun and snow!

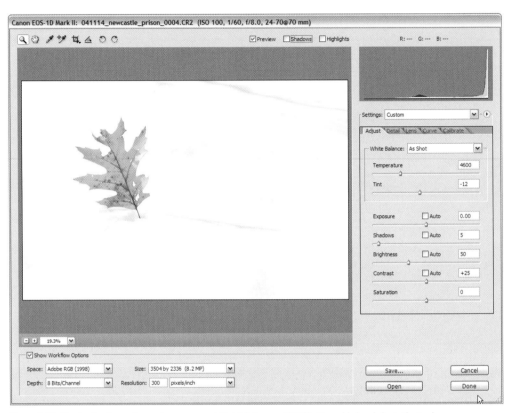

Figure 3.13 The starting image is grossly overexposed. Had this been a JPEG file, it would already be in the trash.

You can see from the histogram that most of the image is against the right side. I turned off clipping highlights for a better view of the image. With the Highlights box checked, everything in the image is red except the leaf.

My first step was to make exposure corrections to see if there was anything that could be recovered. I ended up subtracting almost 2.5 stops of exposure to the image, as shown in Figure 3.14. However, I did recover significant amounts of detail in the snow and fixed the exposure for the leaf quite nicely.

After setting the White Balance and adjusting the Tint to remove the magenta cast, I made adjustments to Shadows and tweaked the Exposure control a bit more. Finally, I adjusted Brightness and Contrast to arrive at Figure 3.15.

Figure 3.14 I made a −2.4 adjustment to Exposure, which helped significantly. Because the White Balance was off, I set this to Daylight, but you can see that the tint is now off.

Figure 3.15 After adjustments are made to the other controls in Camera Raw, the image looks much better and the histogram is now more distributed.

After opening the image in Photoshop, I did a little cleaning up around the leaf and decided to add some punch to the image by changing the color of the leaf to red. Here's the final image in Figure 3.16. There are still blown highlights in the image—Photoshop couldn't completely save me from myself—but the image is vastly better than the original, thanks to the latitude that shooting in RAW provides.

Figure 3.16 Some cropping, cloning, and a bit of creative leaf coloring has resulted in a much better image than the one I took originally.

Using the Shadows Control

The Shadows slider is similar to the slider in the Levels command that is used to set the black point. The control works by stretching the shadow values in your image. By moving the slider to the right, the number of pixels that are mapped to black increases, which can also give the appearance of increased contrast. Although the control ranges from 0 to 100, typical settings for the Shadows slider will be low—often less than 10. As with the Exposure control, the best method of using the Shadows control is by checking the clipping checkbox for obvious telltale signs of loss of detail in the shadows. To prevent more data from being clipped than you want, keep a close eye on the left side of the histogram as you make your adjustments.

Fine-Tuning the Shadows

With the Shadows control, I prefer to leave a bit of extra space to allow for curves and other adjustments after the conversion process. Figure 3.17 shows an image where using the Auto checkbox sets Shadows to 8. The histogram for the image looks pretty good, with image data contained within the boundaries of the histogram. You can see from the preview that some of the black in the egret's legs is showing in blue, indicating that shadow detail is being clipped.

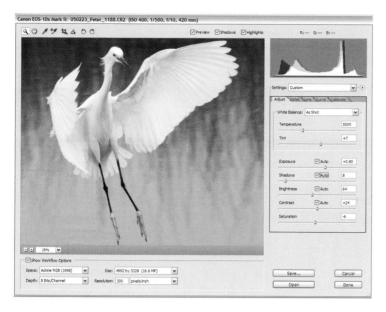

Figure 3.17 The Automatic setting for Shadows in this image is 8. There is some clipping in the egret's legs, but this is acceptable for the subject. (Image courtesy of Peter Burian, www .peterkburian.com)

You can also see that a bit of highlight detail is being clipped at the top of the bird's head and wing. The first step in correcting the image is to reduce the exposure to bring the highlights into range, so I reduced Exposure to +0.65. This let me add just a bit more shadow detail to darken the background a bit. With just an increase of one more shadow point, detail was also added to the egret's wings. Figure 3.18 shows the new settings. Final adjustments were then made to the Brightness and Contrast sliders, as shown in Figure 3.19.

Figure 3.18 Dropping the Exposure just enough to elimi- nate clipped highlights has given the image enough room to increase Shadow detail by 1 point. The amount of shadow data being clipped is affected, but the background is darkened a bit to make the bird stand out more.

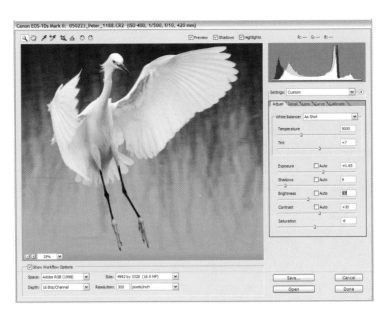

Figure 3.19 After Exposure and Shadows are adjusted, the Brightness control is reduced to eliminate highlight problems, and Contrast is boosted a bit.

The final image, shown in Figure 3.20, has better detail in both the shadows and highlights with more separation of the subject from the background than the RAW file originally had.

Figure 3.20 After the adjustments are made in Camera Raw, the converted image has better highlight detail and stands out from the background.

Making Larger Adjustments

The previous example required only minor changes to get the shadows where they belonged. Some images require more extensive changes to adjust the shadow detail properly. Because noise is more of a problem in the shadows, larger adjustments to lighten the shadows carry the risk of introducing noise into the image. To start off, the image in Figure 3.21 needs a large adjustment to the shadows.

By increasing the Shadows slider to 34, as shown in Figure 3.22, the bird and fish both have better separation between shadows and midtones. They are also separated from the blue sky a bit more.

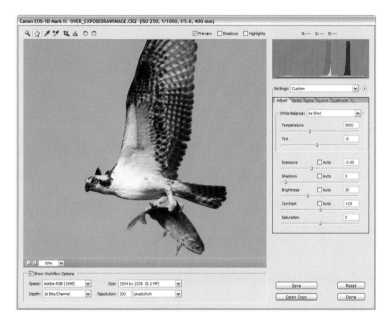

Figure 3.21 A more extreme example, this image could benefit from a large adjustment to the shadows. (Image courtesy of Art Morris, www .birdsasart.com)

Figure 3.22 After the Shadows slider is increased to 34, much more detail and separation exist between shadow and midtone.

The final result, shown in Figure 3.23, has excellent detail throughout the image, with fine shadows and highlights as well as midtones.

 Note: Don't forget the Alt+click/Option+click and slider adjustment combo that changes the preview display to help you determine problems when you are making Shadow adjustments. Holding the key down while dragging the Shadows slider will turn the preview area into a clipping display.

Figure 3.23 After the Shadows slider is increased, the converted image has excellent detail from shadow to highlight.

Using the Brightness Control

Your first impression of the Brightness control might have you wondering what distinguishes it from the Exposure control. By brightening or darkening an image, it does make similar adjustments. However, rather than setting the black and white clipping points, the Brightness control works by compressing or expanding highlight and shadow detail.

> **Note:** The Brightness control should be used *after* Exposure and Shadow adjustments have been made.

This is similar in function to the middle slider in the Photoshop Elements and Photoshop Levels dialog. The image in Figure 3.24 will be used to show the effect of the Brightness control.

To make your image brighter overall, move the slider control to the right. This expands the shadows while compressing the highlights. Figure 3.25 shows the image after this adjustment. You can see by the histogram that the shadows have been reduced, while more of the image data has moved into the center portion of the histogram. Most importantly though, this has opened up the image enough to see detail in the background wallpaper.

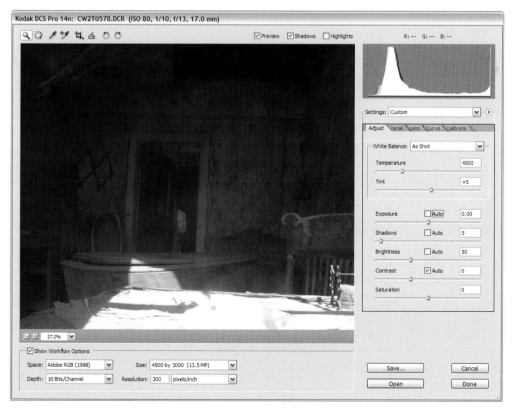

Figure 3.24 This is our starting point for making adjustments to the Brightness control.

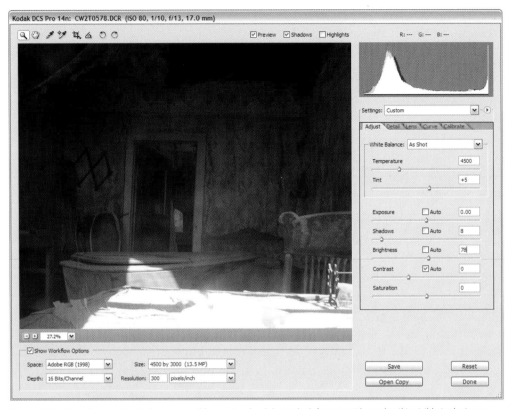

Figure 3.25 After adjusting the Brightness control by moving the slider to the left, more midtone detail is visible in the image.

As with the other controls in Camera Raw, you should keep your eye on the histogram to see how the image data is adjusting. Extreme adjustments will clip highlight and shadow detail, so take it nice and easy as you correct your images.

Note: Some images will begin to show clipping with smaller adjustments as well. It really depends on where the image data was to begin with. Clipping is more of a problem with large adjustments, but keep an eye on the histogram whenever you make these adjustments to your images.

Using the Contrast Control

The Contrast control adjusts the midtones in an image. Photoshop Elements has a Levels control that works in a similar manner, while Photoshop users also have Levels but will likely be familiar with the Curves control, which is a more powerful adjustment tool. Like the Brightness control, Contrast should be adjusted after Exposure and Shadows and normally after Brightness.

Almost all RAW files will benefit from some contrast adjustment. Some images, such as portraits, particularly of women, where smoother skin tones and generally softer features are desired, will use a lower setting.

To increase the contrast in a RAW file, adjust the Contrast slider to the right. Moving the slider to the left decreases contrast in the image giving it a flatter look. In Figure 3.26, The Automatic setting of +19 was too strong for this image and produced harsh shadows on the model's face, so I adjusted the Contrast slider to +3.

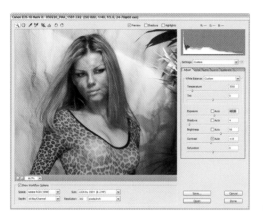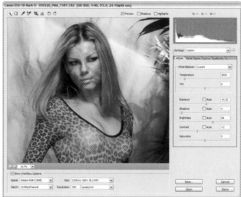

Figure 3.26 (left) The default setting for Contrast on this image was too high and made the midtones appear too harsh on the model's face. (right) Lowering the Contrast setting in Camera Raw corrected the problem.

In contrast (no pun intended) to the previous image, the example shown in Figure 3.27 needed an increase in contrast. The original was a bit flat and had no real definition from shadow to midtone. By increasing the Contrast slider to 52, you give the image a more dramatic look.

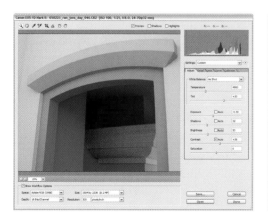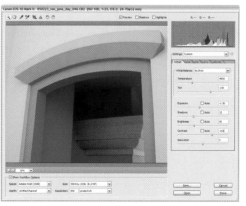

Figure 3.27 (left) The default setting for Contrast on this image was too low and the entire image looks rather flat. (right) Raising the Contrast setting in Camera Raw corrected the problem.

Adjusting Saturation—Not Yet

When first beginning to work with RAW images, many people are surprised by how flat the images look when compared to the JPEGs they have been shooting. The primary reason for this is that JPEG images are already converted when you see them. The camera has made decisions on how much saturation to apply, and more often than not, tends to be optimized for vibrant color.

If saturation needs to be adjusted, I usually prefer to make these adjustments after the conversion using the tools in Photoshop, which give greater control over the process. If adjustments are to be made in Camera Raw, they should be minimal. There is one exception to this rule of thumb though, and it's one that not many people consider—black-and-white conversion in Camera Raw. I'll cover this technique in detail in Chapter 4.

Setting Sharpness

Although Camera Raw includes a Sharpness slider, applying sharpening during the conversion is not the ideal method to use. Because sharpening needs will be specific to each image and the intended output, setting a default sharpness can lead to problems after the conversion. The other reason to avoid sharpening during conversion is that Camera Raw doesn't offer the level of control over sharpening settings that Unsharp Mask does. This can lead to halos and other problems that are nearly impossible to correct after they have been applied.

 N o t e : For more detailed information on sharpening images, I recommend *Photoshop Sharpening,* an e-book by Tim Grey. It's for sale at www.sybex.com.

The problem with turning off sharpening is that your image will appear somewhat soft when displayed in Camera Raw since it is showing the image as recorded, rather than the JPEG preview shown on the camera's LCD. Unlike your RAW file, that JPEG preview has sharpening applied automatically. The best way to deal with this is to use the Sharpness slider only on the preview image.

Photoshop CS2 allows you to apply sharpening to the preview only in the Preferences dialog. This will let you see how your image will look with sharpening applied, but when the conversion is done, it will not be applied to the converted image. To set Camera Raw to use sharpening only on the preview, open the dialog's pop-up menu (under the histogram, next to the Settings list) and choose Preferences. In the Camera Raw Preferences dialog, select Preview Images Only from the Apply Sharpening To list, as shown in Figure 3.28. Click OK to save your changes and return to Camera Raw.

Photoshop Elements users don't have this advantage though, because the version of Camera Raw included in Elements doesn't have a Preferences option. For users of this version, the safest method is to leave the Sharpness slider set to 0. You can make this the default for Camera Raw by setting the slider to 0 and selecting Set Camera Default from the settings menu.

> **Note:** As an alternative, you can use the control during the editing phase and then set it to 0 before converting. I don't always remember to do this, though. The good news is that you can always reconvert the image if needed—yet another reason to love RAW!

I'll cover the basics of post-conversion sharpening in Chapter 7, "Finishing Touches," along with the other common post-conversion options such as resizing and saving your images.

Summary

Once again we've covered a lot of ground in this chapter. Knowing what each of the controls in Adobe Camera Raw does and understanding how they interact with each other are critical parts of the RAW workflow. Camera Raw will allow you to make adjustments to your images that would be impossible or extremely difficult in Photoshop Elements or Photoshop CS. Best of all, Camera Raw makes those adjustments using the full information stored in your RAW file. If you decide you don't like the settings after your conversion, the original RAW file is still available to you, ready for the next experiment.

I hope this chapter has helped you understand how each of the controls works and has shown you how important the histogram is.

Beyond the Basics

4

Now that you have a good understanding of how the major adjustment controls work in Adobe Camera Raw, you're ready to go beyond the basic RAW file conversion and start to tap into the extra power you have with the Camera Raw converter. Using the controls covered in this chapter, you'll be able to tone images, reduce noise problems, and do very good black-and-white conversions—all using the full information in your RAW file. If you find yourself using certain settings frequently, you'll appreciate knowing how to save and use custom settings to accelerate your workflow.

Chapter Contents

Using the White Balance Tool

The White Balance tool ✎ in Adobe Camera Raw works differently than the other white eyedroppers in Photoshop Elements and Photoshop. The eyedropper in Camera Raw doesn't sample the color you click (as the eyedropper in the Tool palette does) nor does it set a white point (like the white eyedropper in the Levels and Curves commands). The Camera Raw eyedropper sets the white balance of the image based on where you click, which is how the center, or gray, eyedropper works in Levels and Curves. In other words, wherever you click the white balance eyedropper in Camera Raw, all three color channels will be set to the same value, making that the neutral reference for your image.

When you click a point in your image, that point determines the color temperature and tint of your image by measuring the color values of the pixels under the eyedropper. The White Balance tool works best on any areas of the image that still contain detail and would look correct if made to be neutral in tone. Figure 4.1 shows the difference between clicking a highlight area with no detail and one with some detail.

Figure 4.1 The White Balance tool in Camera Raw works by setting the temperature and tint of the image based on the point you click. (left) Clicking a highlight area with no detail results in an image that is warmer. (right) When you select an area with some detail in the highlights, the color balance is rendered more accurately.

When you have several possible areas in your image, click each of them to see which selection gives you the temperature and tint you want. Remember that photography is subjective, and within reason there can be multiple correct choices Figure 4.2 shows examples of how different settings could be correct for the image depending on the mood you are trying to present.

Adjusting Color Tint

The Tint slider in Adobe Camera Raw is commonly used to fine-tune the color of your images. By moving the slider to the left, you add more green to the image; adjustments to the right add more magenta. You can also use the Tint slider for some creative effects. This works best with high key images (ones that contain mostly highlights with little tone separation) that you want to give an alternative processing tone to, such as platinum or sepia, and it works best in conjunction with the Temperature slider.

Figure 4.2 Here are variations on a theme. All four of these images use a different white balance as selected by the White balance tool. Any of them could be considered correct depending on the mood I want to convey. Which is best? You decide!

Starting with a high key image open in Camera Raw, adjust the Tint slider in the direction you want the final image to go. To add blue or green tones, adjust to the left. Adjusting the slider to the right will add reds and sepias. Figure 4.3 shows an original as well as three alternatively toned images.

Controlling Noise with Luminance Smoothing

Luminance Smoothing is used to control the noise that appears in some digital images, particularly at higher ISO settings or with long exposures. Luminance noise looks like variations in tone, particularly in the shadow areas of an image, reminding many people of the grain in film. Most images, particularly those shot at lower ISO settings or shorter exposure lengths, will not need any changes to Lumanince Smoothing, so don't plan on applying this to every image you convert.

Using the Luminance Smoothing control is easy enough: anything above zero will begin to remove the random noise. (If you're using Photoshop, this slider is on the Camera Raw Details tab.) The drawback to the control is that some softness will be introduced to the image as part of the correction. To get started, I recommend zooming in to at least a 100 percent preview of the area you are most concerned about, as shown in Figure 4.4.

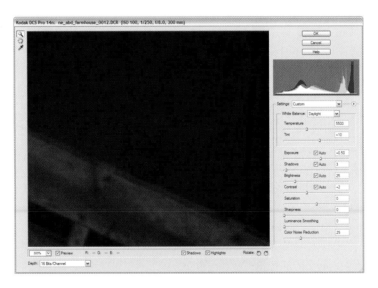

Figure 4.3 You can mimic alternative processing techniques with the Tint slider. This works best with high key images that have little color variation from which to begin. For these examples, I used settings of 0 for the neutral print, −25 for the platinum tone, +40 for the sepia tone, and −60 for the selenium tone print. In all cases, the adjustment was a combination of color temperature and tint.

Figure 4.4

Zoom in as much as possible on the problem area before making Luminance Smoothing adjustments. Because this adjustment softens the image somewhat, you'll want to keep the changes to a minimum.

Note: With the Luminance Smoothing and Color Noise Reduction sliders, I suggest zooming in as much as possible to see just what the noise problems are and how much correction is needed to reduce them. Using the Sharpness slider to make the noise easier to detect might also help; if you do this, be sure to reset the slider to zero before converting the RAW file.

You can make the needed adjustment easier to see by using Camera Raw's Sharpness slider. The additional sharpness, as shown in Figure 4.5, makes the noise more prominent.

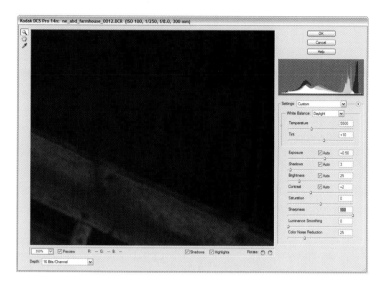

Figure 4.5

Applying sharpening to the image helps the luminance noise stand out more to help with editing.

I find that small adjustments here are normally the best, with many images requiring a value of less than 10, and very rarely up to 15. In the example shown here, I increased the setting to 8, which has reduced the appearance of noise, or graininess in the image, without destroying detail (Figure 4.6).

> **N o t e :** If you are using Photoshop Elements—or you are using Photoshop and didn't take my advice in Chapter 3, "RAW Conversion," to apply sharpening to only the preview—be sure to return the Sharpness slider to zero before converting the image.

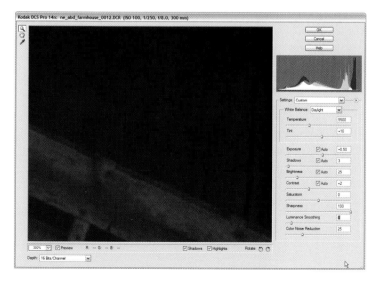

Figure 4.6

After increasing the Luminance Smoothing slider to a setting of 8, the appearance of noise is improved.

Here's the converted image, with and without Luminance Smoothing applied. Compare the shadow areas of the image on the left with the same area on the right (Figure 4.7). There is less random variation in tone with the corrected image on the right. It's a subtle difference here, but in a larger print the change is very apparent.

Figure 4.7 (left) Before and (right) after Luminance Smoothing. Note the differences in the shadow areas. The after image is smoother, with fewer variations in tone.

Controlling Noise with Color Noise Reduction

If you have green or magenta speckles in your image, particularly in dark areas, or you see these speckles around highlights in the image, you are a victim of color noise. The problem is particularly bad at higher ISO settings and with longer exposures. Color noise shows up even more with high-resolution compact cameras that pack more photosites into a smaller area, resulting in sensors that are more sensitive to light than their digital SLR counterparts that use larger sensors.

The method of correcting color noise is very similar to the one used previously for luminance noise. Start off by zooming in as much as needed to see detail in the problem area of your image (Figure 4.8).

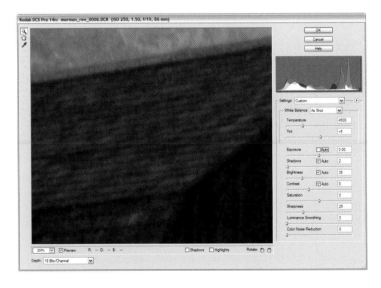

Figure 4.8
After zooming in on the problem area, the color noise problems are obvious in this image. All of the green and magenta splotches are signs of noise.

Color Noise Reduction doesn't have the same problem with affecting the sharpness of the converted image that Luminance Smoothing does, but you'll still want to keep your adjustments to the minimum acceptable here. (If you're using Photoshop, this slider is on the Camera Raw Details tab.) I suggest starting at the control's default setting of 25 and going from there. Again, watching the preview area as you make adjustments, watch for the splotches of color to begin to blend away as shown in Figure 4.9.

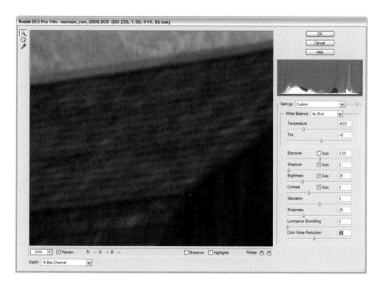

Figure 4.9
Moving the Color Noise Reduction slider to the right begins to blend the green and magenta color spots into the surrounding tones, making the image look less noisy. For this image, I've raised the slider to a setting of 42.

As you can see in the before and after (Figure 4.10) images, the green and magenta problem areas are much less visible in the shadows of the image.

Figure 4.10 (left) Before color noise reduction is applied, there are noticeable problems with noise in the shadows of this image. (right) After the Noise Reduction slider is adjusted, the splotches of color are much less noticeable. This has allowed other minor image adjustments to contrast and brightness to be made as well.

When to Look into Other Tools

To be honest, the noise reduction tools in Adobe Camera Raw don't offer the level of control that will take care of every noise problem you encounter. Some other tools available that can work minor miracles on your noise plagued images are available. These other tools have a couple of drawbacks that you should consider, though. First, they are an extra expense. Second, these programs don't work on the RAW images, so you'll need to do all your conversions first and then run the image, either a TIFF (recommended) or JPEG through their noise-reduction process. Finally, using them adds an extra step in the workflow. With these caveats in mind, I recommend any of the following for those really tough noise problems. Each of the applications listed here works on both Macintosh OS X and Windows XP systems.

Noise Ninja (www.picturecode.com) This includes both stand-alone and Photoshop and Photoshop Elements plug-in versions. The program includes numerous profiles for specific cameras and includes information on how to create your own profiles. Noise Ninja does the best job of luminance noise reduction of any program I've tried. I recommend getting the Pro version, which supports 16-bit images and batch-processing options. The Pro version costs about $80, and it includes the plug-in and the stand-alone version.

nik Dfine (www.nikmultimedia.com) This is a Photoshop and Photoshop Elements plug-in. Dfine has the most intuitive interface of the noise-reduction programs listed here, and it does a particularly good job with color noise reduction. If you use any of the other nik products, such as Sharpener Pro or Color Efex, Dfine will be easy to understand and use. It runs at around $100.

Neat Image (www.neatimage.com) This is the other strong contender for noise reduction. Neat Image and Noise Ninja compete for best results on many images. Neat Image also has a stand-alone and plug-in version of the program. The stand-alone version supports batch processing and 16-bit files. The Windows Pro bundle, which includes both versions, costs under $80; and the Mac version is under $40.

My Recommendation If you frequently find yourself making adjustments to RAW images in Camera Raw but aren't happy with the results, take a look at one of these programs. All three work on Macintosh or Windows systems, and all work with Photoshop Elements and Photoshop. I recommend Noise Ninja. It does the best overall job and is significantly faster than the other options. All of them have free trial versions available, try them out and see which suits your needs best.

Converting to Black and White

Black-and-white photography has been enjoying an increase in popularity these days, in part due to the ease of converting digital images from color to grayscale. Image-editing programs like Photoshop Elements and Photoshop have always supported converting digital images to grayscale, although not always with the greatest results.

Black-and-White Images in Camera Raw

One of the best uses for the Saturation slider in Camera Raw is the conversion to black and white. By setting Saturation to –100, the image is displayed as grayscale. Converting in Camera Raw has its advantages; you have the full data from the RAW file to work with and adjustments to exposure and shadow detail are better handled in Camera Raw than in Curves or Levels in Photoshop or Photoshop Elements after the conversion.

However, a simple saturation adjustment is seldom going to give you a good black-and-white image. In fact, desaturating a color image usually leaves you with a bland, flat-looking image. Most color images require a significant amount of "massaging" to turn them into a good black and white. Serious Photoshop users have learned to master the Channel Mixer control for their conversions, while Photoshop Elements and Photoshop users who only deal with black and white occasionally tend to go with one of the many plug-ins available. You can, however, do a very good job of black-and-white conversion within Camera Raw, and it's not as difficult as you might think.

To make this type of conversion, open a RAW image (Figure 4.11) and move the Saturation slider all the way to the left.

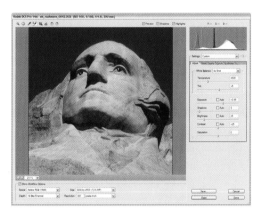 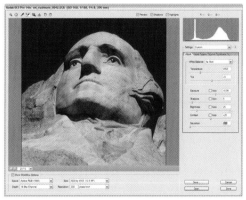

Figure 4.11 This is the image I've selected to convert from color to black and white. (right) After setting the Saturation slider to the far left, I have a basic grayscale image.

The next step is to make adjustments to exposure. Many black-and-white images look better with more defined white points and black points. I find that adjusting the Exposure for the maximum amount of highlight detail works best. To do this, first determine which highlight area in your image has the detail that is the most important to retain. This will serve as the guide for how much exposure you can add to the image. Using the Alt/Option key while adjusting the Exposure control, move the slider until you see the critical highlight area begin to clip, and then back off the slider just enough to eliminate the clipping (Figure 4.12).

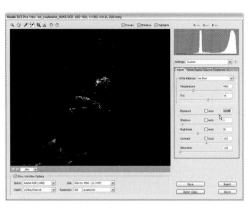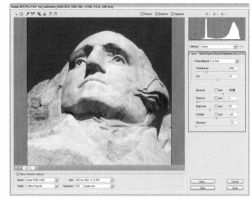

Figure 4.12 The next step is to adjust exposure to set the white values for the image. Start by identifying the critical highlight area of the image. This is the lightest area that you want to retain image detail.

If you are using Photoshop, using the Color Sampler tool can help with this adjustment. Select the Color Sampler tool ✎ and click the highlight area you want to maintain. Now, when you adjust the Exposure with the Alt/Option key, the sample point will be displayed while you make the adjustments so you'll know precisely where you were trying to keep detail.

Adjustments to the Shadows slider will set the black values for the image. Again using the Alt/Option key while making the adjustment, move the slider until you have the blacks set where you want them (Figure 4.13). As with the Exposure control, here you want to maintain detail in the important shadow area of your image.

Depending on the image and the amount of adjustment made to exposure, the Brightness slider may not need to be used at all. In Figure 4.14, I've made a small increase in overall brightness to open the image up a little more. This adjusts the midtones of the image and may or may not be appropriate for the type of image you are converting.

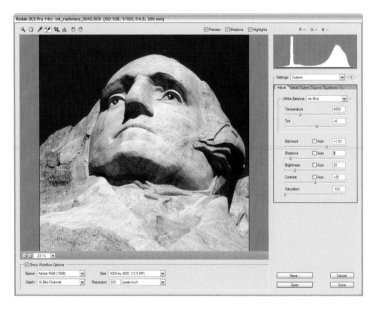

Figure 4.13

After adjusting the shadows to set the black values, the image is beginning to take on a more traditional black-and-white feel.

The final step in the conversion is to adjust contrast. Black-and-white images often need a boost in contrast when compared to the same image in color. In the example image shown in Figure 4.15, I've increased contrast to 38. The final image, shown in Figure 4.16, is now ready for conversion. For a strong black-and-white image with good definition between tones, an increase in the Contrast slider can make a huge difference in the image.

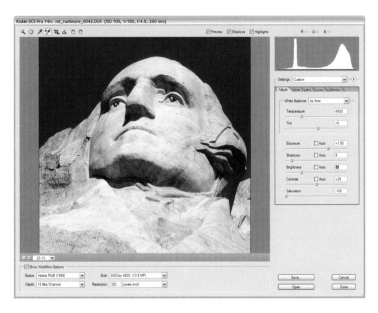

Figure 4.14

A small adjustment was made to the midtones with the Brightness slider.

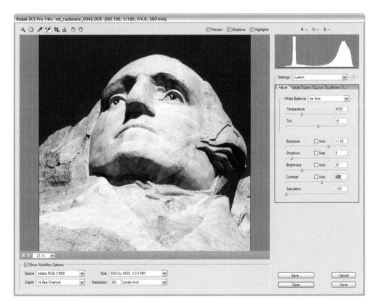

Figure 4.15

Increasing the contrast will often add more depth to a black-and-white image.

Figure 4.16 (left) The image after only desaturation looks very flat in comparison to the final image (right) with further adjustments in Camera Raw.

Advanced Black and White with Calibrate

If you are using Camera Raw with Photoshop, you have even more options available to you. The Calibrate tab can be used in a fashion similar to the Channel Mixer command in Photoshop. You'll start out the same way as the previous example, by reducing the Saturation to zero. After making adjustments to the major adjustment controls, you can fine-tune the black-and-white effect by using the Calibrate sliders.

Next, select the Calibrate tab in Camera Raw. The Red, Green, and Blue Hue sliders work like the corresponding controls in the Channel Mixer control, while the Saturation sliders affect the intensity of the Hue sliders. Unlike traditional black-and-white filters, positive adjustments affect the opposite color. For example, boosting the Red sliders, as shown in Figure 4.17, will darken reds in the image.

Figure 4.17 (left) The image prior to adjustments of the Hue and Saturation sliders. (right) Increasing the Red sliders enhances the rocks and adds contrast to the sky.

Increasing the Greens adds more intensity to green shades, as shown in Figure 4.18, while increasing the Blues to the values shown in Figure 4.19 will lighten the sky.

Figure 4.20 shows the image with all adjustments and some minor post processing edits such as cropping and sharpening.

Figure 4.18 The image after adjusting the Green sliders to enhance the grass.

Figure 4.19 The Blue sliders have been adjusted up, which has darkened the sky and given the foreground subject more emphasis.

Figure 4.20 Here's the final image after cropping and sharpening in Photoshop. It is much better than a simple grayscale conversion.

Saving and Using Custom Settings

Depending on which version of Camera Raw you are using, you can save or reset only the Camera Defaults or a wide range of individual options. Photoshop Elements only lets you save all of your adjustments. If you find that you are making the same adjustments to every, or nearly every, image you convert, you can save a step by making these settings the Camera Default (Figure 4.21). After making adjustments to the sliders, click the triangle next to the Settings dropdown list and choose Set Camera Default. These settings will now be used as the starting point for any new RAW image conversion.

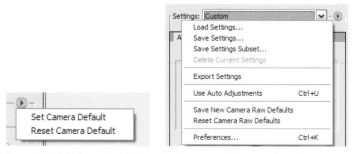

Figure 4.21 (left) Camera Raw in Photoshop Elements only gives you the option to set or reset the default settings. (right) Camera Raw in Photoshop offers a number of other options, including the ability to load and use a subset of the saved settings.

> **Note:** You can return to the original settings by choosing Reset Camera Default from the Settings menu.

Because the camera default affects every setting in Camera Raw in Photoshop Elements, it is most useful when you have a group of images to convert with similar corrections. By correcting the first image and then saving the camera default, you can make the change once. Now, all future images opened will use the adjusted controls.

If you find that images from your camera consistently need a correction in Luminance Smoothing or Color Noise Reduction, making just those adjustments and saving the camera default will apply the new setting to any future images.

Photoshop users of Camera Raw have significantly more options available to them than do users of Photoshop Elements. The ability to save and use subsets of the controls in this version of Camera Raw gives you the ability to create settings that are tuned to specific needs, such as a lens or custom color calibration. These techniques are covered in detail in Chapter 6, " Advanced Conversion Options."

Summary

This chapter has shown you how to fine-tune your image in Camera Raw to correct color balance and noise problems that may exist in the RAW file. Along the way, you've learned how to save custom settings to make recurring adjustments happen automatically. You've seen that Camera Raw can act as a high-quality black-and-white image-conversion program for your RAW images as well. In the next chapter, I'll show you how to put Camera Raw to work for you by automating many of these tasks.

Automating
Camera Raw

When you're looking at hundreds of RAW images, or even a few, the thought of adjusting and converting each of them can be discouraging. Luckily, Adobe Camera Raw has several options available for automating the task. In fact, if you use Adobe Bridge, you don't even need to launch Photoshop!

In this chapter, separate sections are devoted to each of the software combinations (Bridge, Organizer, CR, etc.). You can skip over the sections that don't apply to your setup.

Chapter Contents

Applying Settings

One handy and quick method of updating a set of RAW files is to apply Camera Raw settings without actually converting the images to TIFF or JPEG files. Both Photoshop Elements and Photoshop make the application of Camera Raw settings to multiple files quick and easy.

Why would you want to apply settings without doing a conversion? The most common reason is to apply a set of global changes that multiple files will need, such as white balance correction, without having to apply these settings to each file as you convert it. If you have several (or several hundred) images that all need one or two common corrections in addition to individual adjustments, this is a quick way to make these changes.

Applying from File Browser

Users of Photoshop Elements or of a version of Photoshop earlier than CS2, whether on Macintosh or Windows, can apply settings from File Browser, which is where you'll find the Apply Camera Raw Settings command (hard to miss with a name like that!).

 Note: Photoshop Elements Organizer doesn't include the Apply Camera Raw Settings command, so you'll need to work in File Browser for this.

To get started, open File Browser from within Elements. You'll actually need to open one RAW file in Camera Raw and make all the adjustments needed. This image will serve as the reference image from which all the others will inherit settings. Here are the steps to follow:

1. Navigate to the folder that contains the images you want to update.

2. Select the first RAW image you want to update and double-click it to launch Camera Raw.

3. Make the global changes that every image will need, such as white balance and exposure corrections.

4. Press and hold the Alt/Option key and click the Update button, as shown in Figure 5.1, to apply the changes to that image without converting it. This will save those edits and close Camera Raw, returning you to File Browser.

5. Select the image you just updated, and then select the other RAW images to which you want to apply the new settings. Shift+click to select contiguous files, Ctrl/Cmd+click to select noncontiguous files.

6. On the Macintosh, choose Automate > Apply Camera Raw Settings, which will display the dialog shown in Figure 5.2. On Windows, choose File > Apply Camera Raw Settings. The options on either platform are identical.

Figure 5.1 Holding the Alt/Option key in Camera Raw changes the buttons from Open and Cancel to Update and Reset.

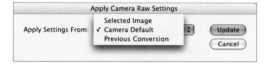

Figure 5.2

The Apply Camera Raw Settings dialog (this is the Photoshop Elements version) lets you select which settings to use for updating your RAW files.

7. Choose First Selected Image and click Update.

All the images you have selected in File Browser will have the settings from the first image applied to them. From here, you can either open individual images in Camera Raw for fine tuning, or you can move to the batch conversion step that I cover later in this chapter.

Other options in Apply Camera Raw Settings will update the files with the previous conversion, which is useful when RAW files live in multiple directories, and Camera Default, which returns the settings in the selected images to the default settings.

> **Note:** Don't confuse Camera Default with As Shot. Selecting Camera Default will apply the settings saved as the defaults that you have when Camera Raw opens a RAW file for conversion. Whatever changes you've made through the Set Camera Default command will be applied to each image. As Shot will apply the settings used by the camera at the time of image capture.

Applying from Bridge

Bridge offers Photoshop users two ways to apply settings to multiple RAW images without converting them. If you've already made changes to one of your RAW files, start by selecting it in Bridge, and then follow these steps:

1. Choose Edit > Apply Camera Raw Settings > Copy Camera Raw Settings, or type Ctrl+Alt+C (Macintosh Cmd+Opt+C).

2. Select the other RAW images to which you want to apply the new settings. Shift+click to select contiguous files, Ctrl/Cmd+click to select noncontiguous files.

3. Choose Edit > Apply Camera Raw Settings > Paste Camera Raw Settings, or type Ctrl+Alt+V (Macintosh Cmd+Opt+V). The Paste Camera Raw Settings dialog, shown in Figure 5.3, opens and displays the options available to you.

Figure 5.3

Paste Camera Raw Settings lets you copy everything or just a single adjustment—the choice is all yours. I've selected the Adjustments Subset in this example.

The Paste Camera Raw Settings dialog lets you pick and choose which adjustments you want to apply. This has come in handy for me on several occasions when I've made more adjustments to an image than I want to apply everywhere. You can either click each checkbox to select or unselect the adjustment, or you can select Subset from the dropdown list and then select the settings you want to apply. When you click OK, the marked adjustments will be applied to all selected images.

The other option for applying settings is similar but more direct. You'll still need to have made changes to one of the RAW images. Rather than copying and pasting settings to other images, select Edit > Apply Camera Raw Settings > Previous Conversion. This is an all-or-nothing choice; you don't have the option to select subsets or individual adjustments.

Note: If you're not happy with the changes, just select Edit > Apply Camera Raw Settings > Clear Camera Raw Settings to revert to the original settings.

Applying in Camera Raw (Photoshop CS2 Only)

Of all the new features in Photoshop CS2, the changes in Camera Raw to support batch processing are the most exciting to me. With this newest release, it's possible to have all your RAW files open in Camera Raw at once for easy selection and modification. As you can see in Figure 5.4, thumbnails for all selected images are displayed in a scrolling panel, called the Filmstrip, on the left side of the Preview area.

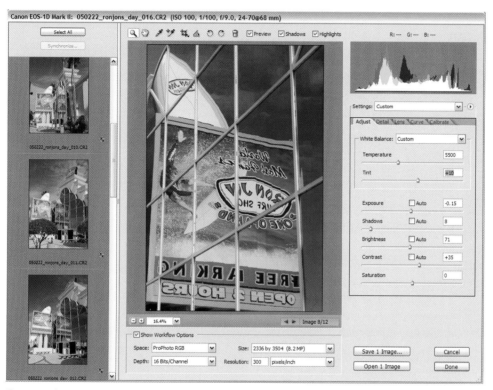

Figure 5.4 The new version of Camera Raw in Photoshop CS2 handles multiple files for quick and easy settings changes.

When multiple files are selected, either via Bridge or through the Photoshop File > Open menu, the Camera Raw interface changes a bit to handle the new features.

The Filmstrip, shown in Figure 5.5, displays a thumbnail for each image open in Camera Raw. Above the thumbnails are two buttons. Select All is pretty obvious. Synchronize is the button that will apply your adjustments to all selected images.

Note: You can work on a subset of images in the Filmstrip by selecting individually or by pressing the Shift or Ctrl/Cmd keys and clicking for multiple files.

Note: You can resize the thumbnail panel by dragging the vertical separator bar between the thumbnails and the Preview area. Larger thumbnails are easier to work with when you are making edits.

Figure 5.5
The Filmstrip displays all RAW files open in Camera Raw. The Synchronize button applies changes to all selected images.

Just below the Preview area are navigation buttons with an image counter (Figure 5.6). This feature lets you move from one image to the next without clicking individual thumbnails. Finally, the buttons for Save and Open (Figure 5.7) change to reflect the number of selected files.

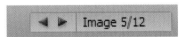

Figure 5.6 The navigation buttons let you move from one image to another.

Figure 5.7 The Save and Open buttons change to show how many images will be affected.

To apply settings from within Camera Raw, start by selecting the images in Bridge, and then choose File > Open in Camera Raw. If you are already in Photoshop, you can select File > Open and select the files you want to modify.

There are two ways to apply changes to multiple files in Camera Raw. The first is by selecting multiple thumbnails and making the adjustments on the first image. Each adjustment you make will be applied to every selected image and the thumbnails will update to reflect the changes.

The second method takes advantage of that Synchronize button. Select the image that you want to use for your adjustments and correct it until you have the settings you want. Now, select all the desired thumbnails and click Synchronize. The dialog box shown in Figure 5.8 will open, letting you select which adjustments to apply to all images.

Figure 5.8

The Synchronize dialog has options to apply all settings or subsets. (It should look familiar; it's the same as the Paste Camera Raw Settings dialog seen earlier.)

After selecting which settings to apply, click OK and all selected images will be updated.

Finally, after all your adjustments have been made, click the Done button to apply the changes and close Camera Raw. Alternatively, you can select Save or Open. Open will launch Photoshop if it isn't already running, launch Camera Raw to apply the changes to your RAW files, and leave the selected files open for post processing. Save does the conversion work for you and saves the files in the selected format without going into Photoshop for editing. I'll cover why you'd want to do that in just a bit.

Converting Images

Of course, the end goal when working with a RAW file is to convert it into a actual image file, whether that is a JPEG for web use or a TIFF for high-quality output such as printing. Converting a single image is straightforward enough: just click the OK button or Open button in Camera Raw and all settings are applied to the image, which is then opened in Photoshop Elements or Photoshop. But, since the theme of this chapter is automating Camera Raw, let's focus on batch, or multiple file, conversions. Both Photoshop Elements and Photoshop support batch conversions, but each does it in a different way.

Converting from File Browser

Photoshop Elements handles batch conversions from within File Browser. All the processing work is done through the Process Multiple Files command, which can convert, rename, and resize your images without opening and saving each one manually.

1. To get started, select File > Browse Folders and navigate to the folder containing the RAW files you want to convert.

2. Select the RAW files you want to convert by Shift+clicking for contiguous files or Ctrl+clicking for noncontiguous files.

3. From the File Browser menu bar on Windows, choose File > Process Multiple Files. On the Macintosh, choose Automate > Process Multiple Files. You'll see the dialog box shown in Figure 5.9.

Figure 5.9 The quickest way for Photoshop Elements users to do batch conversions is to use Process Multiple Files in the File Browser.

For this example, I've already selected the images I want to convert so Process Files From will be left at File Browser. If I wanted to convert an entire folder of RAW files, I'd select Folder. The Import option isn't valid for RAW images, and the Opened Files option implies that you've already converted the images and have them open in Elements.

Destination lets you navigate to the folder you want to use to save the converted images. If you're converting with the Folder option, you can also specify whether to save to a new folder or save to the same folder by checking Same As Source.

File Naming has the same options as the Batch Rename dialog. Refer back to Chapter 1, "Preliminary Workflow," for details on naming options and suggestions.

Image Size gives you the option of resizing your image as part of the conversion process. Unless you have a specific use intended for the converted file, I don't recommend resizing during the conversion. The exception to this is when converting directly from RAW to JPEG for web use. I occasionally convert RAW files for multiple uses by running Process Multiple Files once to save them as 16-bit TIFF files and a second time to create small JPEGs that will be used for a contact sheet. For the second pass, I select Resize Images and set a Width of 320 and leave Constrain Proportions checked.

File Type has a number of options available, but you'll want to select TIFF for normal conversions. This converts your images at 16-bit (if selected in Camera Raw) for the most color information possible.

> **N o t e :** If you convert files to JPEG, they will be saved as 8-bit images regardless of the setting in Camera Raw.

In general, I don't recommend using the Quick Fix settings in Process Multiple Files. There are exceptions to this of course, which I'll discuss later in this chapter.

Converting from Organizer (Windows Only)

Organizer has a very limited form of batch conversions. In fact, it really isn't a batch at all but an interactive way to open multiple RAW files for editing. File Browser is a much better way to convert multiple RAW images, but it can be done through Organizer if you feel the need.

1. To get started, launch Organizer by clicking Photo Browser ⟲▦ Photo Browser in the Photoshop Elements toolbar.

2. Select the RAW files you want to convert by Shift+clicking for contiguous files or Ctrl+clicking for noncontiguous files.

3. Next choose Edit > Go To Standard Edit. This will open Adobe Camera Raw with the first image. If you've already made your corrections in File Browser, just click the OK button to convert the image. Camera Raw will automatically open the next selected RAW file, continuing until all selected images have been converted. Organizer displays a lock icon over the images that are selected for conversion, as shown in Figure 5.10, and a lock with the text Edit In Progress for images that have been converted and opened in Elements.

If you haven't applied settings to the RAW files you're opening from Organizer, the quickest method is to make the adjustments to the first image and then select Previous Conversion from the Camera Raw Settings dropdown list.

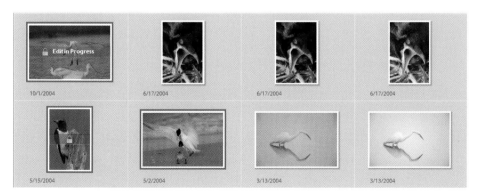

Figure 5.10 Organizer tracks which images are selected for conversion with a banner and lock icon. (Images courtesy of Art Morris, www.birdsasart.com)

The final checkbox in Process Multiple Files is Log Errors, which creates a text file list of any errors that occurred during the conversion process. I suggest leaving this option checked so that you have a reference to any possible errors. Unchecking the option will ignore any errors that occur.

Converting from Camera Raw (Photoshop CS2 Only)

I've already covered how to apply settings to multiple files from within the Photoshop version of Camera Raw. To perform the actual conversion, you simply need to select the files in the Filmstrip and click Save, as shown in Figure 5.11.

This will display the Save Options dialog, shown in Figure 5.12, which has several settings for the converted files, including where to save the file, what to rename the images, and what type of conversion to perform.

Destination options are to Save In Same Location or Save In New Location. Clicking Select Folder will automatically change the dropdown list to Save In New Location.

File Naming has the same options available as the Batch Rename command, which was covered in detail in Chapter 1.

Figure 5.11 To batch convert the selected images in Camera Raw, click Save.

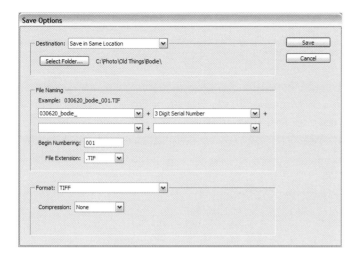

Figure 5.12
You'll specify where to put the converted files and to which file type you want them converted.

Format offers several options, including Digital Negative, TIFF, and JPEG. You'll typically want to save as TIFF in order to take full advantage of the 16-bit color space. Selecting JPEG will automatically convert your files as 8-bit regardless of the Depth setting in Camera Raw. If you do select JPEG, you have the option to set Quality; I recommend setting this to Maximum for best results.

Once you click Save, all images will be converted and saved in the specified location. As the images are processed, a not-very-obvious status link is displayed above the Save button (Figure 5.13). Clicking this link will open a Camera Raw Save Status dialog (Figure 5.14) showing which files have been processed and as what type. If you want to cancel the conversion, click the Stop button in this dialog.

Note: Holding the Alt/Option key while clicking Save bypasses the Save Options dialog. The Save Options from the previous conversion will be used if you bypass the dialog.

Figure 5.13
Camera Raw shows the number of files being converted. Clicking the link opens the Save Status dialog showing the progress of the batch conversion

Figure 5.14 To cancel a batch conversion, click the Stop button in the Camera Raw Save Status dialog. This dialog also shows which files have been converted and to what file type.

Quick Fix Settings

The Process Multiple Files dialog in Photoshop Elements has a nifty feature that you might be considering. The Quick Fix and Labels checkboxes on the right will apply the Auto settings and Sharpen after the image has been converted. Here's my advice on using these settings: **DON'T!** At this point, you've already made the correct adjustments in Camera Raw so there's no point in letting Elements decide to change things around. Sharpen should never be used, and certainly not at this point in the workflow.

Note: Don't confuse Sharpen with Unsharp Mask. Sharpen is an automatic application of the filter with no control over settings. Unsharp Mask, on the other hand, gives you full control over how your image is sharpened.

You can use the Labels option to place text directly on your images. It's sort of like the date imprints from some of point-and-shoot film cameras. Do you really want text plastered onto your image? Probably not. However, you might want to mark your images when converting them for web use. In that case, a copyright notice might be appropriate (Figure 5.15).

Figure 5.15

The only time I would use the Labels option during conversion would be to place a copyright notice on an image destined for the Web.

To place a copyright notice, select Watermark from the dropdown list. In the Custom Text field, enter the text you want to appear in the converted image. Select a position, either Bottom Left or Bottom Right (unless you want to be bold and place your text in the center of your image), and then set the Opacity and color of your text.

Note: To insert the copyright symbol ©, press Opt+G (Macintosh) or Alt+0169 on the numeric pad (Windows).

Resizing Images: Now or Later

The odds of using your image files at their native size run a close second to winning the lottery. Almost every image you take is going to be made larger or smaller for its intended use, whether that be a print or for web display. All Adobe Camera Raw users can automate the resizing task during the conversion process by using the appropriate options in the Process Multiple Files command. Users of Photoshop also have the option to resize selected images in Camera Raw.

If you know in advance that you'll be using a particular image at a certain size, Camera Raw does a very good job of image resizing. Figure 5.16 shows the same image resized to the same dimensions. The image on the left was resized in Camera Raw, while the image on the right was resized in Photoshop using Bicubic Smoother.

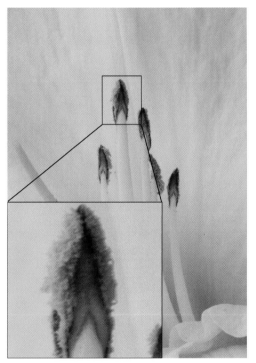
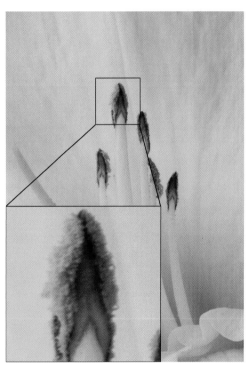

Figure 5.16 (left) This image was resized in Camera Raw as part of the conversion process. (right) The same image was resized in Photoshop after conversion. There is very little difference in quality between the two images.

Note: If you use the Nikon D1x or Fuji S2, you'll have better results by resizing one step up in Camera Raw, with any additional resizing done in Photoshop. That's because these cameras use pixels that are not square and Camera Raw can resize for the maximum quality.

The Photoshop version of Adobe Camera Raw includes a Size option below the preview area shown in Figure 5.17. The Size dropdown has several preset sizes with the default being the RAW file's native size. Depending on the resolution of your camera, you'll see different options and perhaps even different numbers of options, as shown in Figure 5.18. For example, the Canon 1D Mark II has seven sizes listed with three smaller, native, and three larger; the Kodak SLR/c and Canon 1Ds Mark II have more options to reduce the file than enlarge.

Figure 5.17 The Size list in Photoshop's version of Camera Raw lets you resize the image during conversion, saving a step later in the workflow.

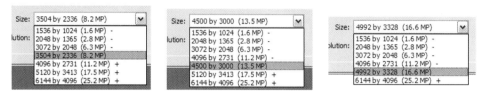

Figure 5.18 (left) Depending on the resolution of your camera, the size options will vary. Here the sizes are for the 8.2 MP Canon 1D Mark II, (center) the 13.5 MP Kodak SLR/c, and (right) 16.6 MP Canon 1Ds Mark II.

As you can see, the preset size options remain nearly constant. The possible choices are 1.6 MP, 2.8 MP, 6.3 MP, 11.2 MP, 17.5 MP, and 25.2 MP, although not every option will be seen with every camera. (For instance, the 17.5 MP option isn't available with the Canon 1Ds Mark II, and the 6.3 MP option won't be seen with Nikon D70 RAW files).

For the most flexibility, I prefer to resize after the conversion. Of course, if you are using Photoshop Elements, this is the only option available to you unless you are using Process Multiple Files, which makes the decision a bit easier. I would rather resize one time for the best possible quality. Because any resizing will resample the image, it's best to avoid multiple sizing operations when possible.

Using Actions (Photoshop CS2 Only)

In the case of Photoshop, I've only touched on what is possible with automation. Actions, which are recorded tasks, can be used to handle complex operations such as saving in multiple formats. If you've used macros in other programs, such as Word or Excel, you have an idea of what Actions are.

Note: For even more advanced options, CS2 comes with several prebuilt scripts (found under File > Scripts); if you have some programming skills, you can also write your own. For an idea of what scripting can do, visit the Adobe website (share.studio.adobe.com/) and select Scripts from the listbox for information and samples.

The Actions palette in Photoshop, shown in Figure 5.19, is where you'll record and access your Actions. For this example, I'm creating an Action that will do the following:

• Open the RAW image using the current Camera Raw settings.

• Save the image as a 16bit TIFF file in the destination folder.

• Convert the image to the sRGB color space.

• Resize the image to fit within a 800×600 size.

• Convert the image to 8 bits.

• Save the image as a JPEG file with a quality level of 10.

To get started, I suggest creating a new Action Set for your RAW conversion actions by clicking the Create New Set icon . Storing all related Actions in a set help you organize and find them when they are needed, and it helps you hide them when you don't need them.

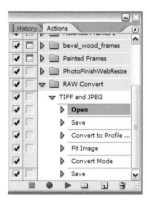

Figure 5.19
You'll create and run recorded tasks in the Actions palette in Photoshop.

Next, click the Create New Action icon to begin recording your Action. The dialog shown in Figure 5.20 is displayed. Give your new Action a descriptive name, and click the Record button.

Note: You can assign a function key to the Action, which will be handy if run the Action frequently. This lets you start the Action from the keyboard rather than selecting it from the palette and clicking the Run button.

Figure 5.20
Once you click Record in the New Action dialog, everything you do in Photoshop is recorded for future playback until you click the Stop button.

Once you start recording, everything that you do in Photoshop will be saved to the Action for future playback until you click the Stop button. For this example, I'm saving the image twice. The first save is a 16-bit TIFF file, while the next save converts the file to 8 bit, resizes it for web use, and saves it as a high-quality JPEG. The completed Action, shown in Figure 5.21, will perform these same operations on every file I want, and much faster than I can do it manually. In this example, I've specified the folder I want to save to. This means the Action will always save to this folder. You can change the destination in the Batch dialog if you wish by selecting Folder in the Destination list and navigating to the new folder.

Figure 5.21
The recorded Action is a list of all of the commands performed during the recording.

To run the Action, you have two choices. You can click the Run icon to run the Action on a single file. However, the second option is where automation with Actions really shines. Select File > Automate > Batch to display the dialog shown in Figure 5.22. From Batch, you can run the same Action on a folder of files or a set of opened images.

Note: You can also run your Action from Bridge. Select Tools > Photoshop > Batch. This launches Photoshop and opens the Batch dialog.

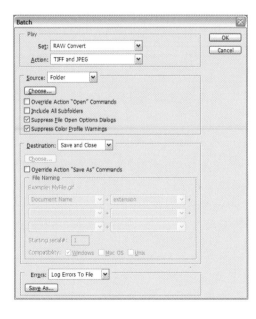

Figure 5.22
The Batch command takes Actions to the next level by working with multiple files to perform the same commands on all of them.

Select the Set and Action from the dropdown lists and then select the Source. If you want to convert an entire group of files, select Folder; otherwise if the files have been opened or selected in Bridge, select Opened Files.

When you check the Suppress File Open Options Dialogs and Suppress Color Profile Warnings boxes, Photoshop will open the files without prompting for user input, which would create an error.

Choose None for Destination to save the files to the same location. When you click the OK button, your Action will run on every selected file, whether you've selected two files or thousands.

Note: If your Action changes a file without renaming it, I recommend setting the Destination to a new folder and saving a copy of the file. Selecting None will overwrite the original file if the same name is used. To choose a new folder, select Folder in the Destination drop down list, then click Choose to navigate to the folder you wish to save the converted files in.

Summary

Whether you have two files or two thousand that need to be edited, using the batch processing features in Camera Raw, Bridge, Photoshop, and Photoshop Elements can help make the job easier and more consistent.

Advanced Conversion Options

This chapter is just for those of you using Adobe Camera Raw in Photoshop CS2. This version of Camera Raw offers many more controls over RAW image processing than the Camera Raw (CR) in Photoshop Elements or even in earlier versions of Photoshop. Don't get me wrong—Elements and Camera Raw are a powerful combination that can handle most RAW file conversion tasks. However, when you need advanced controls, or you are processing hundreds and thousands of RAW files on a regular basis, you'll quickly appreciate the extra features found here.

Chapter Contents
Fixing Chromatic Aberration
Adjusting Vignetting
Using the Curves Control
Calibrating Camera Raw
Cropping and Straightening
Creating Custom Settings
Saving in Camera Raw

Fixing Chromatic Aberration

Chromatic aberration is the term used to describe that "lovely" color fringing, or colored halos, seen on some images, particularly in high contrast areas of the image. It's more problematic with zoom lenses, and it is made worse by the sensitivity of digital sensors. Figure 6.1 shows an example of chromatic aberration. Chromatic aberration occurs when all of the light wavelengths coming through the lens don't align precisely at the same point, in this case the sensor in your camera.

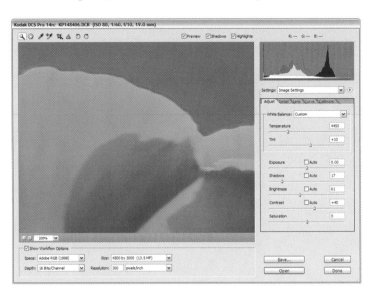

Figure 6.1
Chromatic aberration rears its ugly head as color fringing. It is especially noticeable around high contrast areas of an image.

Camera Raw has two sliders to help correct chromatic aberration, located on the Lens tab (Figure 6.2). The first, Chromatic Aberration R/C, adjusts red/cyan fringing problems, while Chromatic Aberration B/Y adjusts blue/yellow fringing problems. Both controls work by adjusting the amount of red and blue compared to the amount of green.

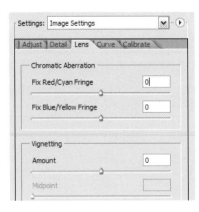

Figure 6.2
The adjustment sliders for chromatic aberration are located on the Lens tab of Camera Raw. Separate sliders control Red/Cyan and Blue/Yellow color fringing.

Note: If you're wondering why only the red and blue are adjusted, remember that photosites have red, blue, and green filters. The Chromatic Aberration sliders work by adjusting how strong the reds and blues are by adding or subtracting those colors.

Enough with theory! How about a real example? The California poppies in Figure 6.3 show strong chromatic aberration along the edges of the flower petals.

Figure 6.3

The original image shows strong chromatic aberration on the edges of the flowers. This is easy to correct in Camera Raw.

To start, open the image in Camera Raw and make any major adjustments such as Exposure, Shadows, and Contrast. To help with your adjustments, turn Sharpening off in the Detail tab. This will make it easier to tell what is actually chromatic aberration and what is an artifact of sharpening.

By holding down the Alt/Option key while clicking each of the Chromatic Aberration sliders, you can hide the other color channel to make it easier to see where the problem areas are. In Figure 6.4 there is an obvious problem in the Blue channel while the Red/Cyan channel looks fine.

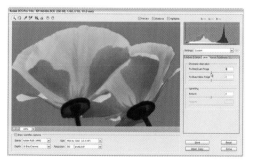

Figure 6.4 (left) Holding down the Alt/Option key while clicking the Fix Red/Cyan Fringe slider hides the Blue channel and shows that this image has no fringing problems that need correcting in this channel. (right) The same Alt/Option+click combination on the Fix Blue/Yellow Fringe slider shows strong chromatic aberration along the edge of the flower petals.

Don't be afraid to drag these sliders large amounts if needed. Unlike adjustments to noise, there is little, if any, image degradation or softening when using the Chromatic Aberration controls. The image in Figure 6.5 needed to have a +55 adjustment to the Fix Blue/Yellow Fringe slider to correct the fringing problems.

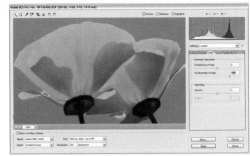

Figure 6.5 (left) A fairly large adjustment of +55 to the Fix Blue/Yellow Fringe slider has reduced the color fringing in this image to an acceptable amount. (right) The adjusted image with all color channels visible shows a much cleaner edge along the flower petals.

Seeing exactly what has changed may be difficult. A side-by-side comparison of the image should help you see the greatly improved definition between flowers and sky. Figure 6.6 shows the original along with the corrected image.

Figure 6.6 (left) Before the Chromatic Aberration is corrected, the image has color fringing along the edges of the flowers. (right) After the correction, the definition between flower and sky is much better.

Adjusting Vignetting

Vignetting, or darkening of the edges, is a fairly uncommon problem for most digital cameras. It occurs when the light hitting the edge of the sensor isn't as strong as the light hitting toward the center. It's more likely to occur at wide apertures and with full-frame sensors such as the Kodak Pro SLR and Canon 1Ds.

Correcting Vignetting

The Vignetting control is located in the Lens tab, just below the Chromatic Aberration sliders (Figure 6.7). It has two adjustments: Amount and Midpoint. Amount controls how much lightening is added to the corners of the image, while Midpoint controls how wide of an area is affected by the controls.

Figure 6.7
The Vignetting controls are found on the Lens tab. Sliders control the Amount and Midpoint of the adjustment. (Unless the Amount is set to a value other than zero, the Midpoint slider is disabled.)

Figure 6.8 shows a typical example of vignetting in a RAW file. It's most obvious in the upper corners of the image as a darkening of the sky. To correct this, you need to adjust the Amount slider to the right.

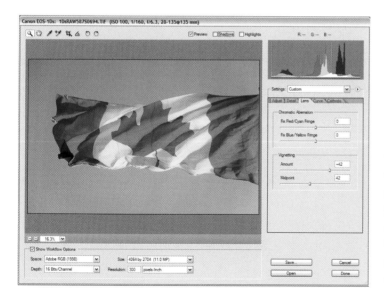

Figure 6.8
This image illustrates a typical vignetting problem. The corners are a little darker than the rest of the image. They can be adjusted with the Amount slider of the Vignetting control in Camera Raw. (Image courtesy of Peter Burian, www.peterkburian.com)

By increasing the Amount slider to 45, the darkening has been removed and the sky now has an even tone from edge to edge (Figure 6.9).

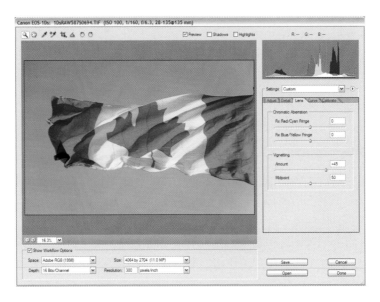

Figure 6.9
Adjusting the Amount slider to 45 has eliminated the vignetting in this image.

The default setting for the Midpoint slider is 50. Lowering the slider by moving it to the left will apply the Amount adjustment to a larger area of the image. Increasing the value by adjusting to the right reduces the area affected by the Amount adjustment. Figure 6.10 shows the difference between the two settings. Your goal is to keep all changes to a minimum, only adding enough Amount and Midpoint adjustment to reduce the vignetting to an acceptable amount.

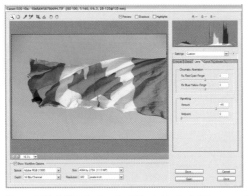 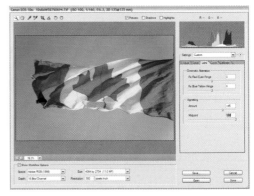

Figure 6.10 (left) Adjusting the Midpoint to the left increases the area affected by the Amount adjustment. (right) Higher Midpoint adjustments confine the Amount adjustment to a smaller area.

Note: You may not be able to completely correct vignetting in the RAW file without making the image unacceptably light. A little experimentation will give you an idea of how much correction a particular image can handle.

The final image, after levels and cropping in Photoshop, is shown in Figure 6.11.

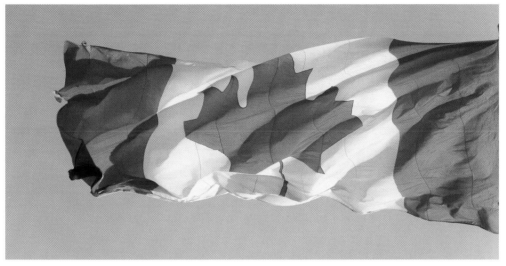

Figure 6.11 The end result has corrected all vignetting that was seen in the original image without affecting the remainder of the image.

Getting Creative: Adding Vignetting

Vignetting correction doesn't always have to be about removing it. Adding vignetting to an image is a creative technique that is used to add an "old feeling" or to draw the viewer's attention toward the middle of a picture. This can be done in Photoshop as well by using a graduated fill adjustment layer, but it's much simpler to do it in Camera Raw with the Vignetting control which is found on the Lens tab.

The image used in this example is from Bodie, California (Figure 6.12). I had to shoot through glass and, as you can see from the color version, this didn't help the image. With a "can't hurt a broken image" philosophy, I decided that a little experimentation with grayscale and vignetting was in order.

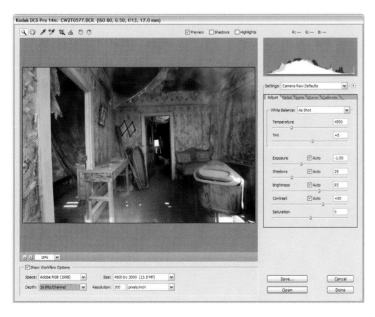

Figure 6.12

The RAW image is unusable as is. The glare and reflections from shooting through an old window made this image either a candidate for creative editing or the trash can.

To start with, I reduced Saturation on the Adjustments tab in Camera Raw to –100. (This technique was covered in Chapter 4, "Beyond the Basics.") This made the reflections less visible and already improved the image. Adjusting the Calibration sliders to +100 Blue Saturation, +100 Blue Hue, –25 Red Hue, and –39 Red Saturation, and boosting the shadow tint a little, resulted in the image shown in Figure 6.13.

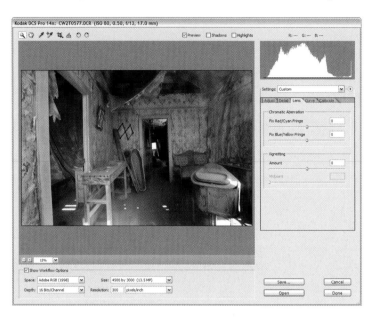

Figure 6.13
Desaturating the image and making adjustments to the Calibration sliders gives the image a good black-and-white feel that looks quite a bit better than the original.

Next, I wanted to darken the edges to give it a vignetted look similar to many old photographs. A setting of –60 to the Vignette slider with the Midpoint slider lowered to 15 looked right for this example (Figure 6.14). The image was now ready for conversion so I clicked Open.

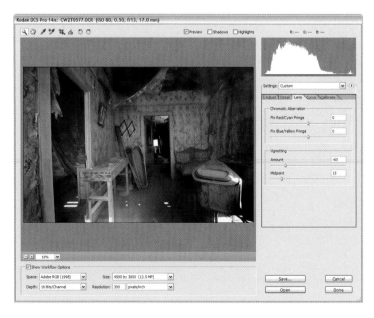

Figure 6.14
After adjusting the Vignetting Amount and Midpoint sliders to darken the corners, the image looks aged.

The final step was to give the image a nice sepia tone. For this, I selected Image > Adjustments > Photo Filter and chose Sepia from the Filter list, as shown in Figure 6.15. Increasing the Density, or strength of the filter, to 57 percent gave the image its final toning. The end result is shown in Figure 6.16. The result is digital lemonade from a digital lemon!

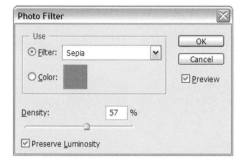

Figure 6.15
The Sepia Photo Filter was selected to give the image a toned look.

Figure 6.16 The finished image took advantage of the problems in the original RAW file to create a photo that appears old.

Note: For full information on black-and-white conversions from Camera Raw, see Chapter 4.

Using the Curves Control

If the adjustments made with Exposure, Brightness, Shadows, and Contrast on the Adjust tab aren't quite what you want, the next stop will be the Curves tab, shown in Figure 6.17. The Tone Curve dropdown includes four preset options:

Linear No additional contrast adjustment is performed on the RAW file prior to conversion. This method is used by the Photoshop CS/Photoshop Elements 3 version of Camera Raw.

Medium Contrast This is the default setting for Camera Raw. It adds a little bit of contrast and is well suited to most RAW images.

Strong Contrast This adds more contrast to the RAW image. It works for some images, particularly images with strong bold lines, but it is not a good choice for portraits or softer images.

Custom You can add and move points along the curve to create your own contrast settings. Any adjustment from the three other presets on the Tone Curve will automatically change the setting to Custom. Up to 14 points can be created.

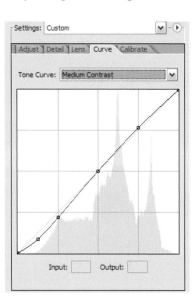

Figure 6.17

The Curves control in Camera Raw can fine-tune adjustments to shadow, highlight, and midtone areas.

Note: Readers who are interested in staying on top of the hottest new features should consider downloading and installing the latest version of Camera Raw. Among future improvements, it will add support for more of the latest camera models and it might include new tone curve settings.

The Curves control shows a tone curve over a histogram of image data. The tone curve is used to adjust the image shadow, highlight, and midtones in a precise manner, similar to the way Curves works in Photoshop. The real power of using Curves in Camera Raw is that you are making these changes on the RAW data, giving you more latitude with any adjustments made.

As with the Curves control in Photoshop, upper right is highlight data and lower left is shadow data. Raising the tone curve by dragging it up from the current position will lighten the pixels in that color range. Dragging the line down will darken the corresponding pixels.

White point and black point can also be changed by dragging the vertical lines to the start of image data on the histogram. Dragging the left line sets the black point, while dragging the right line will set the white point.

To clear a point from the tone curve, click on it and drag it off the control.

Note: To select a specific tonal value, hold down the Ctrl/Cmd key while moving the mouse over the preview area. The tone curve will show where that color value is on the curve. Clicking will place a point on the curve at that value.

The image in Figure 6.18 is close to what I want, but it is still a little flat, especially in the clouds. In order to adjust the image, I want to modify the curve to darken the midtones with more control than the Adjust tab gives me.

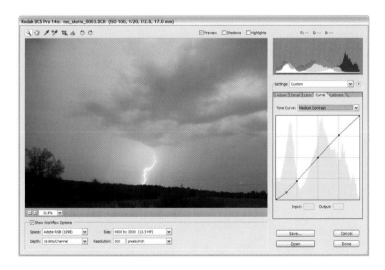

Figure 6.18
The clouds in this image don't have the menacing look I remember from taking the image. Even after making adjustments to exposure, shadows, and contrast, I want to fine-tune the image.

When you hold down the Ctrl/Cmd key while moving the mouse pointer over the image preview area, a dot will display on the curve that corresponds to that color value. This makes it easy to select exactly the points on the tone curve to adjust. The main area of adjustment is in the midtones, which I've darkened by dragging the points below the line as shown in Figure 6.19.

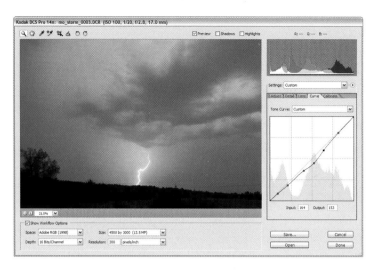

Figure 6.19
After adjustments to the tone curve are made, the clouds have much more impact without affecting the rest of the image.

Calibrating Camera Raw

Camera Raw can be calibrated, or adjusted, to match unique lighting situations or, if you're really having problems, your individual camera. The controls on the Calibrate tab, shown in Figure 6.20, make it possible to adjust the saturation and hue of each color channel as well as the shadow tint.

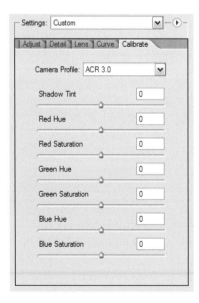

Figure 6.20
The Calibrate tab in Camera Raw enables you to correct for color casts in an image or for your specific camera.

Depending on your camera model and version of Photoshop, the Camera Profile list may contain any or all of the following choices:

Embedded The profile contained in the RAW file.

ACR 2.4 The profile that was provided with the Photoshop CS/Photoshop Elements 3 version of Adobe Camera Raw.

ACR 3.0 The built-in profile included with the Photoshop CS2 version of Camera Raw.

Adjusting Shadow Tint

Adjustments to Color Temperature and Tint will sometimes create a color cast in the shadow areas of your image. The Shadow Tint slider is used to correct this problem. Although it varies depending on the color cast, the slider usually adds green when moving left, or negative, and magenta when moving the slider right, or positive. Figure 6.21 shows both of these adjustments.

Figure 6.21 (left) The Shadow Tint slider corrects color casts that can be created when adjusting the Temperature and Tint controls. Negative numbers typically add green. (right) Positive numbers add magenta to the shadows.

Adjusting Hue and Saturation

In Chapter 4, and earlier in this chapter, I used the Hue and Saturation sliders on the Calibrate tab to adjust black-and-white images. A more common use for these controls is to correct color images, removing any color cast from each of the channels that may be present in your RAW captures.

I suggest adjusting Hue first and modifying Saturation only if needed.

Use the Hue and Saturation sliders to adjust the red, green, and blue in the image. Look at the preview image as you make adjustments until the image looks correct to you. In general, adjust the hue first and then adjust its saturation. Moving the Hue slider to the left (negative value) is like a counterclockwise move on the color wheel, and moving it to the right (positive value) is like a clockwise move. Moving the Saturation slider to the left (negative value) desaturates the color, and moving it to the right (positive value) increases saturation. Figure 6.22 shows an image from the Badlands that needs some calibration help. The colors are flat, with too much red, and the green hue is off.

After the adjustments are made, the image (as seen in Figure 6.23) is much more accurate in color. Because the camera used to shoot this image tends to have a similar overcast-lighting problem with landscape-type photos, I saved the settings to reuse for other similar images. I'll cover saving settings later in this chapter.

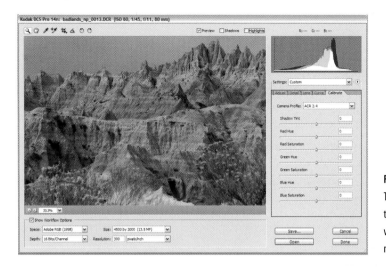

Figure 6.22
This image needs some calibration help. All three colors are off, with too much red and green and not enough blue.

Figure 6.23
After adjustments are made to the Hue and Saturation sliders, the color in the image is much more accurate than the original RAW image file.

Cropping and Straightening

Cropping and straightening in Camera Raw have two main advantages over doing the same operations after conversion. First, it's one less step to perform later. Second, it reduces the file size of the open image. When you are looking at file sizes of up to 95MB (in the case of a Canon 1Ds Mark II converted to 16-bit TIFF), the file size savings can be well worth the time to crop in Camera Raw.

Camera Raw offers two tools for cropping. The first is the conventional Crop tool, which works just like the Crop tool found in Photoshop's toolbar. The second is the Straighten tool, which crops your image while rotating it to straighten a horizon or other line in the image. See Figure 6.24 for a well cropped image.

Note: If the image is too small after cropping, you can use the Size control to resize the image prior to conversion. The Size list box will show the current size with the selected crop area.

Figure 6.24
A well cropped image contains only the elements that are important. This image by Kelly Michele Storer is an excellent example of cropping. There is no wasted space in this photograph. (Photograph courtesy of Kelly Storer © 2004)

The Crop Tool

Cropping is pretty straightforward: You drag a selection rectangle around the part of the image you want to keep. If that was really all there was to cropping, it wouldn't be worth discussing here, though, would it?

The Crop tool hides some helpful goodies behind its dropdown menu, as shown in Figure 6.25. To access the menu, click and hold the mouse button on the Crop tool until it displays.

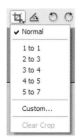

Figure 6.25
The Crop tool can make life easier for you when you resize your image for a specific output need.

By default, six options are available. Normal is a free-form crop: whatever you drag out on the preview is what you'll get with no resizing applied to the converted image. The other options are all aspect ratios; 1 to 1 is square, 4 to 5 is 25 percent longer in length or width than the other dimension, etc. Like Normal, these choices don't resize the image on conversion, but they do ensure that the dimensions will fit into these standard formats when you resize in Photoshop.

The Custom option will save you some time and effort if you know in advance that you'll be using a RAW file for a particular use. When you choose Custom, the dialog box shown in Figure 6.26 is displayed.

Figure 6.26
The Custom Crop option makes it possible to create cropping presets that fit your needs.

Clicking the Crop dropdown list allows you to select the type of crop you want to create: Ratio, which is what the presets use, or a specific size in pixels, inches, or centimeters (Figure 6.27). These final three choices will resize the image to match the dimensions you select for the custom crop.

Figure 6.27
You can create a new crop based on Ratio, like the presets, or a custom size crop that will resize the image on conversion.

For this example, I've created a custom crop of 11×14 inches. Once the custom crop is created, it will be listed in the dropdown menu for the Crop tool (Figure 6.28).

Figure 6.28
After a custom crop is created, it will be displayed in the dropdown menu for the Crop tool.

 Note: If you create a custom crop, it will be selected in the dropdown menu by default.

When this 11×14 crop is selected, any area that I drag out with the Crop tool on the Preview window will be automatically sized to 11×14 inches when converted. To reflect this, the Workflow Options area of Camera Raw is updated to show the crop size rather than the dimensions in pixels (Figure 6.29).

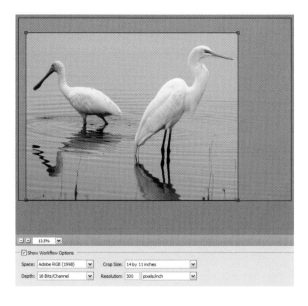

Figure 6.29

When a custom crop for a specific size is used, the Workflow area of Camera Raw updates to show Crop size rather than pixel dimensions.

After dragging out a cropping selection, you can modify the crop by dragging the handles in the corners of the selection. Moving the mouse pointer over the selection handle displays a double-ended pointer . Any resize will keep the same dimensions (if anything other than Normal is selected from the menu). Moving the mouse pointer just outside the handles will show a curved arrow pointer that lets you rotate the selected crop as shown in Figure 6.30.

Note: The Rotate tool is similar to the Straighten tool, which is covered next, with one exception: it only changes the rotation of the crop, not the size of the selection.

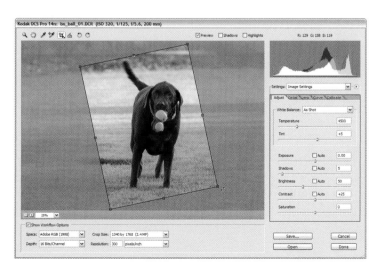

Figure 6.30

Use the Rotate tool to correct a tilt or to just be creative.

When the crop selection is rotated and opened in Photoshop, the image is rotated to match the angle shown in Camera Raw (Figure 6.31).

Figure 6.31
After the RAW file is converted, it will be rotated to match the crop lines in Camera Raw.

Note: Unlike Photoshop—where you can extend the crop area beyond the actual size of the image—in Camera Raw the selection can't extend past the image boundaries.

The Straighten Tool

The Straighten tool is a shortcut that can be used to correct horizons or other angle problems in the RAW file. The tool can be used either horizontally or vertically and will always create a crop that is as large as possible for the corrected image.

To use the Straighten tool, begin with a crooked image (kind of makes sense doesn't it?) and find a reference in the image that should be straight. Click and drag out a line as shown in Figure 6.32.

The length of the line doesn't matter; the crop will always be as large as possible given the angle of the line. When you release the mouse button, the image will be cropped and rotated as shown in Figure 6.33.

Figure 6.32
Drag out a line with the Straighten tool using a reference in the image that should be straight.

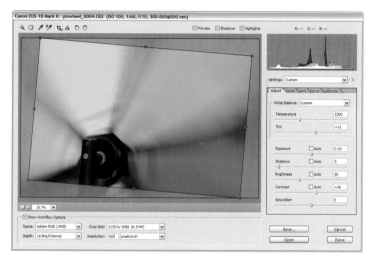

Figure 6.33
After the mouse button is released, a crop will be created that is as large as possible with the selected angle.

Creating Custom Settings

Photoshop CS2 Camera Raw has custom setting options that aren't available in the version of Camera Raw included with Photoshop Elements 3. The options to create custom settings are located in the pop-up menu next to the Settings dropdown list (Figure 6.34).

Depending on the option selected in Preferences (Figure 6.35), settings will be saved as an XMP "sidecar" file or within the Camera Raw database. I strongly recommend using the XMP sidecar option. This way if you move images, or if the Camera Raw database becomes corrupted for some reason, you still have all of your settings.

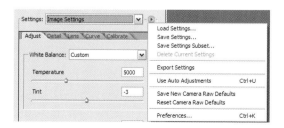

Figure 6.34
All of the custom settings options are located in the pop-up menu next to the Settings list.

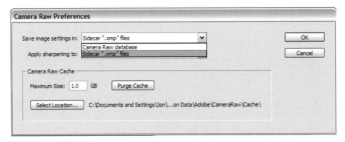

Figure 6.35 The Camera Raw Preferences dialog lets you select whether to store settings in a separate XMP file or in the Camera Raw database.

 N o t e : XMP files are formatted text files that contain the settings information you select.

Changing Camera Raw Defaults

Selecting Save New Camera Raw Defaults updates all settings and makes them the default for any new image opened in Camera Raw. This option works exactly like the one in Photoshop Elements version of Camera Raw. If you constantly make the same changes to your RAW files before converting them (for example, choosing a particular bit depth or turning Auto settings on or off), changing the defaults in this way makes sense. That isn't usually the case though, which makes the other options more attractive and useful.

Saving Settings

Rather than changing the default for all images opened in Camera Raw, selecting Save Settings accomplishes a very similar task but with more flexibility. Save Settings lets you create new named sets of defaults, making it quick and easy to apply several changes at once to an image. This can be very useful when shooting under controlled lighting situations where you might have custom white balance and tint settings, but you don't want to make these adjustments each time.

Saving Subsets

Save Settings Subset, shown in Figure 6.36, is the perfect way to create groups of settings for special situations. Earlier in the chapter, I showed an example of modifying the Hue and Saturation sliders in the Calibrate tab. Since this particular camera always needs a similar adjustment for the same lighting situation, I saved the Calibrate settings as a subset named Kodak Landscape Cloudy. The Subset dropdown list has quick selection options for each of the control sets in Camera Raw. Alternatively, you can click and choose which settings you want to save.

Other Settings Menu Options

Load Settings opens a standard File Open dialog. If you save your settings files to the default location, you won't need to use this option, as the custom settings will show up

Figure 6.36 Save Settings Subset is a great way to create special groups sof settings for reuse.

in the Settings dropdown list. If you saved the file somewhere else, use Load Settings to find the file with the.xmp extension and open it.

Delete Current Settings removes the active custom setting. To use Delete Current Settings, select the custom setting in the Settings dropdown menu to activate it, and then select Delete Current Settings. This will remove the XMP file, so use it with care!

Export Settings will move settings from the Camera Raw database to an external XMP file. If you've set your preferences to save to XMP as I recommended earlier, this command won't be needed.

Use Auto Adjustments will toggle the Auto Adjustment settings on the Adjust tab on or off depending on their current state. If you saved Camera Raw Defaults to turn Auto Adjustments off, this is a quick way to restore them for a RAW file. The Auto Adjustment settings also control how Bridge displays RAW thumbnails.

Reset Camera Raw Defaults will restore all settings to their original state. If things get too funky, sometimes it's best to just start over.

Saving in Camera Raw

New to Camera Raw with Photoshop CS2 is the ability to save converted files without actually opening them in Photoshop. Although this ability is the most useful when converting multiple images, selecting Save rather than Open can be a quick way to do the basic conversion work now while saving the post processing tasks for later. For detailed information on using Save, refer to Chapter 5, "Automating Camera Raw."

Summary

The advanced version of Camera Raw contains a number of additional features geared toward the pro or high-volume shooter. It will also appeal to anyone who likes to tweak settings to get an image just right (Hello, my name is Jon, and I'm a tweaker). All of these options are designed to give you the highest quality image possible before conversion, with the least amount of effort required after the conversion. Still, there are some things that are best left until later, and I'll cover those in the next chapter.

Finishing Touches

RAW is a fantastic way to capture images and retain a high level of control over how the images are processed. As good as RAW is, there are still some things that are better left until post conversion or are possible only after conversion. This final chapter will look at some of the most important post-conversion edits that help put the final polish on your images.

Chapter Contents
Adjusting Output Levels
Removing Dust
Increasing Dynamic Range
Resizing
Sharpening
Saving as TIFF
Saving as JPEG

Adjusting Output Levels

Making a Levels adjustment after converting the RAW image might seem odd. In fact, it shouldn't be necessary with proper adjustment in Camera Raw (refer to Chapter 3, "RAW Conversion," for details on adjusting exposure, shadows, brightness, and contrast).

However, the Levels control is useful for making adjustments to *output* levels, particularly for printing where the printer can't match the shadow and highlight detail of the screen image. By adjusting the slider below the levels graph, you modify the black point and white point for the output device.

As with all image edits, I recommend using adjustment layers whenever possible to avoid changing the master image. To adjust output levels, choose Layer > New Adjustment Layer > Levels.

For most inkjet printers, I recommend setting the Output Levels shadow slider at 10 to prevent shadow detail from blocking up and setting the highlight slider to 250 to avoid clipping in the highlights as shown in Figure 7.1. This slightly reduces the contrast in your image and prevents blank areas in the highlights that may look odd due to the paper color, since areas with a value of 255 have no ink and let the paper show through.

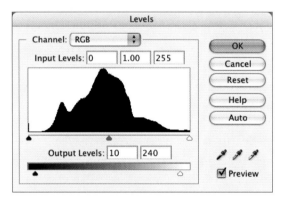

Figure 7.1
To avoid clipping with most inkjet printers, adjust the output shadow and highlight sliders at the bottom to 10 and 250, respectively.

Removing Dust

Anyone who uses a digital SLR with more than one lens will have problems with dust on their images. Note that I say *will*—there is no way around it, although some cameras, such as the Olympus, have hardware features to reduce the problem.

When you view your images in Camera Raw, the telltale dark spots, more obvious in areas with little or no detail such as sky, are sure signs of dust on the sensor. Although you can't eliminate them in Camera Raw before conversion, Photoshop Elements and Photoshop have two tools that help clean them up after the conversion:

Spot Healing Brush tool This is usually the best method of cleaning up dust. Select a brush size from the Options bar that is close to the size of the dust spot, and leave Type set to Proximity Match. When you click the dust spot, Photoshop will replace the area under the brush with color values that match the surrounding area.

Clone Stamp tool When the dust bunnies are too big, or you find what looks like a hair in your image, the Clone Stamp may be your best bet. This tool works by sampling an area of the image and duplicating it as you paint with the tool.

> **Note:** The Healing Brush is a cross between the Spot Healing Brush and Clone Stamp. Like Clone Stamp, it works by sampling an area. However, it uses the sampled pixels to blend with the existing ones rather than directly replacing the pixels. I recommend using Spot Healing whenever possible.

Increasing Dynamic Range

If you've recently switched from print film to digital, you have probably realized that digital images don't have the same dynamic range or ability to capture detail from shadow to highlight as film negatives. Where negative film can record as much as eight stops of light or more, digital is closer to transparency film with a range of about five stops.

There are two ways to increase the dynamic range in your digital images. The first is to use two copies of the same image with one adjusted for shadow detail and the other for highlights in Camera Raw, and combine them in Photoshop Elements or Photoshop after the conversion. The second method is to capture two or more images of the same scene with different exposure settings and combine them after conversion, also in either version of Photoshop. The steps for both methods are essentially the same so I'll use the more common situation, working with only one image. (I won't tell you how long it took me to begin taking multiple exposures at different settings. Let's just say that I learned how to work with one image for this technique.)

To create an expanded range image from the same exposure, open the RAW file in Camera Raw. Figure 7.2 shows the starting point for this example. With Shadow and Highlight clipping enabled, the blue and red show that data is being clipped at both ends of the image. The first conversion will be optimized for shadow detail. Using the Alt/Option key while adjusting the Exposure slider, raise the exposure by moving it to the right until no clipping is seen in the Preview area (Figure 7.3). At this point, the highlights are going to be totally blown out, but don't worry about that for now.

Figure 7.2 Here's the original image. Fixing the shadows will blow out the highlights, and adjusting for the highlights will cause the shadows to go black.

Figure 7.3 The first copy of the RAW file is optimized for shadow detail before conversion. The clipped highlights will be corrected in the second copy.

Make corrections to Shadows, Brightness, and Contrast, as shown in Figure 7.4, and then convert the image by clicking OK (Photoshop Elements) or Open (Photoshop).

Figure 7.4
Make all additional adjustments in Camera Raw to get the maximum shadow detail possible.

 Note: Photoshop Elements users must convert the image to 8 bit for these techniques. Choose Image > Mode > Convert to 8 Bits/Channel if you converted as a 16-bit file.

The second copy of the RAW image will be optimized for highlight detail. Open the same image in Camera Raw. Using the Alt/Option key technique described above, drag the Exposure slider to the left until highlight clipping is eliminated. Once again, the image will show clipping, this time in the shadows. Once again, ignore the clipping because you are only worried about highlight detail in this copy of the image.

After making corrections to Shadows, Brightness, and Contrast the image will look like Figure 7.5. Convert the image with the OK or Open buttons.

Figure 7.5
The second copy of the RAW file is optimized for highlights. Lost shadow detail isn't a concern here; it will be recovered when the images are combined.

Now the fun and magic starts. Just follow these steps:

1. Select the window with the darker of the two images. Choose Edit > Select All (Ctrl/Cmd+A), and then choose Edit > Copy (Ctrl/Cmd+C).

2. Now select the window with the lighter image, and choose Edit > Paste (Ctrl/Cmd+V). If you look at the Layers palette, you'll see two layers (Figure 7.6). The Background is the lighter image, and Layer 1 is the darker image.

Figure 7.6

The Layers palette shows both versions of the file and is now ready for optimizing.

Note: You can close the darker image to free up memory. All edits will be performed on the combined image.

At this point, the two programs differ. The next step for Photoshop users is to add a layer mask to Layer 1. Photoshop Elements users should skip this Step 3 and go down to the alternative Step 3 that follows Figure 7.10.

3. With Layer 1 selected in the Layers palette, click the Layer Mask icon at the bottom of the palette. Layer 1 will then have a white rectangle next to the thumbnail, as seen in Figure 7.7.

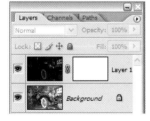

Figure 7.7

After adding a Layer Mask, a white rectangle is shown next to the thumbnail for Layer 1.

4. Select the Background in the Layers palette, and copy it with Select > All and Edit > Copy.

5. Press the Alt/Option key, and click the white rectangle in Layer 1. The image looks like Figure 7.8.

6. Select Edit > Paste. Both the Layer Mask icon and the image window will have a black-and-white version of your image, as seen in Figure 7.9.

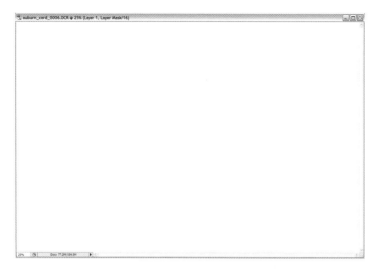

Figure 7.8
After copying the Background and selecting the layer mask, the image will be all white.

7. For the final step, select Filter > Blur > Gaussian Blur, and set a radius of 30. (This is personal preference, but I find that 30 is a good starting point and works for many images. Some images may need much less or quite a bit more. You'll need to experiment to determine the right level for the image you're working on.) Select the Background, and your image will look like Figure 7.10.

Figure 7.9 After pasting the Background into the layer mask, a black-and-white version of the image will be displayed.

Figure 7.10 After applying a Gaussian Blur and selecting the Background, the combined image shows a much wider dynamic range than the original images.

Photoshop Elements doesn't have layer masks, so combining images takes quite a bit more work. Steps 1 and 2 are the same as with the Photoshop method. However, in Elements, you need to erase dark areas of the image to reveal the highlights. By changing the Opacity of the eraser, some of the dark will be left, building density in the image. Photoshop Elements users should follow these alternative steps:

3. After copying the dark image to a new layer of the light image, make sure Layer 1 is selected in the Layers palette.

4. Select the Eraser tool and lower the Opacity to 45 percent in the Options bar. Select a brush size that will work with the area you want to erase, and erase the areas in which you want to restore light detail.

Note: Alternatively, you can use the Selection Brush or Magic Wand ✦ to create a selection before using the Eraser tool. This will confine any erasing to the selected area. Select the area of your image that you want to modify and then make your edits.

The final result takes a steady hand but can do a good job at creating an image with much better dynamic range (Figure 7.11).

Figure 7.11
After being edited in Elements, the final image has a wider dynamic range than the original images.

Note: Photoshop CS2 adds a new feature, High Dynamic Range (HDR), which makes the process of merging multiple images easier. However, it does require more preparation when shooting. To get the most from HDR, you need to shoot multiple tripod-locked images (three to seven, depending on the dynamic range in the scene), each at a different exposure one stop apart. (I recommend using Aperture priority to keep a fixed depth of field and changing the shutter speed.) Choosing File > Automate > Merge to HDR will let you select the images and then create a high dynamic range image that contains all the detail possible. The files are 32 bit and must be converted for printing or other use. For more information, I recommend *Photoshop CS2 Savvy* by Romaniello and Kloskowski (Sybex, 2005).

Resizing

I covered how to resize images using the Photoshop CS2 version of Camera Raw during the conversion process in Chapter 5, "Automating Camera Raw." In Chapter 6, "Advanced Conversion Options," I discussed resizing images when using the Crop tool. You may remember from that discussion that I discouraged resizing during the conversion process unless you had a specific use for the converted image.

Most images don't fall into this category though, so you'll most likely find yourself resizing in Photoshop Elements or Photoshop. Both applications use the same method and dialog, as shown in Figure 7.12.

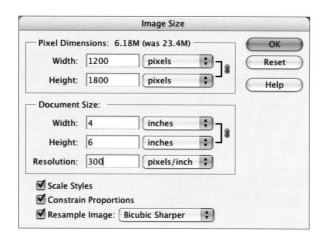

Figure 7.12
Image Size is used after the conversion to resize an image file for a specific use.

To access this dialog, choose Image > Resize > Image Size (Photoshop Elements) or Image > Image Size (Photoshop).

For printing, enter the Width or Height in the Document Size fields for the final print. For web or screen use, enter a Width or Height in the Pixel Dimensions fields.

 Note: If you leave Constrain Proportions checked—and I recommend that you do to avoid distorting the image—set the important dimension, either width or height. The other dimension will be set automatically.

Resample Image offers several options. For photographic images, there are only three options that will give good results.

Bicubic is the standard method and does a good job for most images.

Bicubic Smoother is the best choice when *enlarging* images and will do the best job of interpolation when adding pixels to create a larger image.

Bicubic Sharper is a good choice when *reducing* image size. This option can oversharpen a image, though, so if the resized photo appears too sharp, use standard Bicubic.

Sharpening

Back in Chapter 3, I discussed sharpening in Camera Raw and I recommended that you wait until all image edits and resizing were done before applying any sharpening to your converted RAW files.

Photoshop Elements and Photoshop offer several options to sharpen images, all of which are found under Filters > Sharpen. The chief one that I recommend using, though, is Unsharp Mask. This filter gives you complete control over how your images are sharpened and can be adjusted for different needs.

 Note: For more detailed information on sharpening images, I recommend *Photoshop Sharpening,* an e-book by Tim Grey. It's available at www.sybex.com.

Unsharp Mask

The name Unsharp Mask might sound a bit odd. After all, you want to sharpen the image not unsharpen it, right? Unsharp Mask works by increasing the contrast along the edges in your image, as shown in Figure 7.13, thereby increasing the appearance of sharpness. Don't think of this as a magic tool, though. It isn't going to make an out-of-focus photo look sharp, but it will make your images look more defined by increasing the contrast around the edges.

Figure 7.13 (left) Before applying Unsharp Mask, the image doesn't display strong contrast between the edges. (right) After Unsharp Mask, the edges are more defined, giving the appearance of sharpness.

Unsharp Mask offers three controls for determining how the image is sharpened. **Amount** determines the strength of the contrast added to the edges. Images with high levels of detail will typically use a higher Amount setting of 150 percent or more.

Radius determines how wide the halos that are added to the edges to enhance the contrast will be. Radius is the most critical setting in Unsharp Mask, and it will have lower numbers, usually under 1.0 for high detail images and higher numbers for lower detail subjects.

Threshold controls how much difference there must be between pixels before they are considered edges. High detail images will use lower settings here, because you want more of the image to have defined edges. Values in the 0 to 4 range are common here. Portraits on the other hand will have large areas that you don't want to sharpen, such as skin tones, so you'll use a higher Threshold setting, with 8 or more being common.

Smart Sharpen (Photoshop CS2 Only)

Photoshop users also have the new Smart Sharpen filter. Selecting Filters > Sharpen > Smart Sharpen gives you access to this new filter (Figure 7.14), which has the benefit of more control over how the image is sharpened. Using the new controls in Smart Sharpen, you can adjust how shadows and highlights are affected as well as how blurring is reduced in your image.

Figure 7.14
The new Smart Sharpen filter includes a number of features that make it a useful alternative to Unsharp Mask.

By default, Smart Sharpen starts in Basic mode, which has controls for Amount and Radius that work in the same way as the Amount and Radius controls in Unsharp Mask. The new feature in Basic mode is Blur Removal. Clicking the Remove list box shows three options:

Gaussian Blur is the default and uses the same method as Unsharp Mask.

Lens Blur is the most useful for photographs, and it controls how edges and textures are detected to maintain higher detail in those areas.

Motion Blur would be used to control the angle of correction. Selecting Motion Blue activates the Angle control. This setting is most effective for images that have a small amount of camera or subject movement.

The Advanced option adds Shadow and Highlight tabs to the dialog. Both tabs work in an identical manner on their respective areas and have three controls:

Fade Amount controls how much the sharpening should be reduced in the shadows or highlights. Zero is no reduction at all, while 100 will have the effect completely removed from the shadows or highlights.

Tonal Width determines how wide of a range of tones will be affected by sharpening. Lower numbers will remove the sharpening effect from only the darkest or lightest areas, while a higher number affects a wider range of tones. In general, I suggest keeping this slider at or below 50 for both shadows and highlights.

Radius works in a similar manner to the Radius slider on the Sharpen tab. However, rather than looking for contrast between edges, it determines how wide of an area to use when deciding what the shadow or highlight area is.

I suggest checking the More Accurate option for the best results. It does increase the amount of time needed to apply sharpening to the image, but the end result is worth the time.

Finally, if you find yourself frequently using the same adjustments, you can save them for future use by clicking the Disc icon next to the Settings list.

Saving As TIFF

When all your efforts to produce the ultimate image from your RAW image are complete, you'll obviously want to save your changes. Saving as a TIFF file will give you the most flexibility and retain all of the quality contained in your image. If you do your edits with adjustment layers (and I recommend you do so), saving as a TIFF file will retain the layers, making adjustments for other uses later much easier.

> **Note:** Why not PSD? At one point, PSD was the only way to save files with layers. Now that TIFF supports layers, I recommend saving as TIFF for wider compatibility with other applications and for future compatibility if the PSD format changes.

After selecting TIFF as the file type, the Options dialog offers several choices, as shown in Figure 7.15.

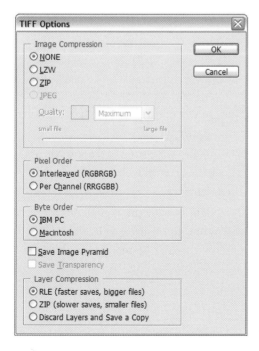

Figure 7.15

The TIFF Options dialog offers a number of settings for your file, including compression and layers.

Image Compression can reduce the size of the saved TIFF file. This can be helpful when you're working with 16-bit files and saving with Layers. LZW offers the most compatibility between applications that support TIFF. I don't recommend using JPEG compression because it is a *lossy* format, or one that throws away information from the image, reducing image quality. ZIP uses the compression format popular on Windows computers, and it will generally result in the smallest TIFF file; however, it may have more compatibility problems. For the best compatibility, select NONE, which will result in the largest file sizes but can be read by any program that opens TIFF files.

Byte Order doesn't really matter these days. If you use a Windows computer, select IBM PC. Macintosh users should select Macintosh. This option defaults to the platform you are working on and was more of an issue in the earlier days. Macintosh and Windows write bytes in the opposite order of each other, and although this used to be a problem going from one platform to another, most programs now understand both orders.

Save Image Pyramid and **Save Transparency** are used by other programs to take advantage of special features in the TIFF file. Image Pyramid provides multiresolution information, which is useful for some applications such as page layout programs that can use a lower-resolution version of the image. Transparency saves the additional information, or alpha channel, for use in other programs. Elements and Photoshop always use the highest resolution image and retain transparency.

Layer Compression will compress data for each layer rather than having to flatten the image. These options will only be available if the image contains multiple layers. RLE will generate the largest size, but it opens much faster than ZIP. The final choice will flatten your image and save a copy.

Saving As JPEG

Saving your image as JPEG implies two things. First, you're willing to save with 8 bits of information rather than 16 bits. Second, you're willing to throw away some image information. (Saving as JPEG will reduce the file size by throwing out information.) The more compression, the more information you lose.

For saving your master files for archiving, I recommend using TIFF. For web or screen display though, JPEG is the file format of choice. For web use, I suggest using a setting of 7 or 8 as a good compromise between file size and image quality (Figure 7.16). For Format Options, Baseline is the standard method. Progressive can be useful for websites because it displays the image in multiple passes filling in detail with each pass. The Size option will estimate the file size after saving and show an estimate of how long it will take to download.

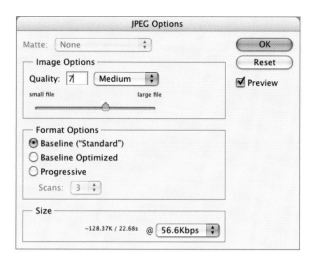

Figure 7.16
JPEG Options determine the amount of compression used and how the image will be displayed. For most images, I recommend a setting of 7 or 8.

The other option for JPEG is Save For Web (File > Save For Web). Save For Web gives you a side-by-side preview of the image before and after compression. It also lets you resize images (Figure 7.17). Save For Web is designed to work with files that are sized for screen use. Trying to use Save For Web with a full-size image may give you a warning message about low memory and slow performance. I've never had Photoshop crash because of this, but when they say slow performance, they mean it! If you see this message when selecting Save For Web, click No and resize the image. Alternatively, just use Save As and select JPEG.

Figure 7.17
Save For Web offers a number of features for saving as JPEG, including the option to resize images and see a before and after preview.

Note: For detailed guidelines on saving images for multiple uses, I recommend my previous book, *Photo Finish*, also by Sybex.

As with the standard JPEG Save dialog, a setting of 70 or 80 will give you a good compromise between image size and quality.

 Note: By default, Save For Web removes any profile associated with the image. If you want to retain your profile, be sure to check the ICC Profile checkbox.

One advantage (or disadvantage, depending on your point of view) is that Save For Web strips out all EXIF metadata from the file. If you don't want someone to know what camera you used, or the settings, this will get rid of the data for you.

Summary

Throughout this book, I've shown you ways to get the most from your digital captures by using the RAW file format. I hope the journey was a fun and educational one and that you're excited to get out and start shooting in RAW to see how much more you can wring out of your digital photos.

Photography is all about creativity for many of us, and by shooting in RAW, you extend your creative control even further. I hope you'll give RAW a try and see how it can help your images.

Appendix: Keyboard Shortcuts

This table shows the keyboard shortcuts available while working in Camera Raw.

Windows	Macintosh	Photoshop Elements 3	Photoshop CS2
Delete	Backspace		When Crop tool is active: Clear crop In Curve tab: Delete selected points on curve In text field: Delete selected text In Filmstrip mode: Toggles "mark for delete"
Escape	Escape	Exit Camera Raw (same as Cancel)	Exit Camera Raw (same as Cancel) When Crop tool is active: Clear crop
Enter	Return	Exit Camera Raw via default button	Exit Camera Raw via default button When Crop tool is active: Switch to Zoom tool
Alt+OK button	Opt+OK button	Update	
Alt+Cancel button	Opt+Cancel button	Reset	Reset
Tab	Tab	Move to next control	Move to next control
Shift+Tab	Shift+Tab	Move to previous control	Move to previous control
Ctrl++	⌘++	Zoom in preview	Zoom in preview
Ctrl+-	⌘+-	Zoom out preview	Zoom out preview
Ctrl+Alt+0	⌘+Opt+0	Zoom to 100%	Zoom to 100%
Ctrl+0	⌘+0	Fit preview to window	Fit preview to window
Ctrl+Z	⌘+Z	Undo/redo last	Undo/redo last
Ctrl+Alt+Z	⌘+Opt+Z	Undo multiple	Undo multiple
Ctrl+Shift+Z	⌘+Shift+Z	Redo multiple	Redo multiple
Ctrl+Shift+A or Ctrl+D	⌘+Shift+A or ⌘+D		Select primary image
Ctrl+0	⌘+0		Open
Ctrl+Alt+0 or Alt+Open button	⌘+Opt+0 or Alt+Open button		Open a copy
Ctrl+S	⌘+S		Save
Ctrl+Alt+S or Alt+Save button	⌘+Opt+S or Opt+Save button		Save with previous settings (no dialog)
I	I	White Balance tool	White Balance tool
Z	Z	Zoom tool	Zoom tool
H	H	Hand tool	Hand tool
C	C		Crop tool
A	A		Straighten tool
S	S		Color Sampler tool

Windows	Macintosh	Photoshop Elements 3	Photoshop CS2
R	R	Rotate right	Rotate right
Ctrl+]	⌘+]		Rotate right
L	L	Rotate left	Rotate left
Ctrl+[	⌘+[		Rotate left
Arrow keys	Arrow keys	Adjust selected slider	Adjust selected slider In Curve tab: Adjust selected curve point In Filmstrip mode: Select image
P	P	Toggle Preview checkbox	Toggle Preview checkbox
U	U	Toggle Shadows checkbox	Toggle Shadows checkbox
O	O	Toggle Highlights checkbox	Toggle Highlights checkbox
Alt+Shadows slider	Opt+Shadows slider	Show Shadows clipping in preview	Show Shadows clipping in preview
Alt+Exposure slider	Opt+Exposure slider	Show Highlights clipping in preview	Show Highlights clipping in preview
Ctrl+~	⌘+~		Clear all stars
Ctrl+1	⌘+1		One star
Ctrl+2	⌘+2		Two stars
Ctrl+3	⌘+3		Three stars
Ctrl+4	⌘+4		Four stars
Ctrl+5	⌘+5		Five stars
Ctrl+6	⌘+6		Red label
Ctrl+7	⌘+7		Yellow label
Ctrl+8	⌘+8		Green label
Ctrl+9	⌘+9		Blue label
Ctrl+Shift+0	⌘+Shift+0		Purple label
Ctrl+,	⌘+,		Remove one star
Ctrl+.	⌘+.		Add one star
Ctrl+'	⌘+'		Toggle one star
Ctrl+Alt+1	⌘+Opt+1		Adjust tab
Ctrl+Alt+2	⌘+Opt+2		Details tab
Ctrl+Alt+3	⌘+Opt+3		Lens tab
Ctrl+Alt+4	⌘+Opt+4		Curve tab
Ctrl+Alt+5	⌘+Opt+5		Calibrate tab
Ctrl+Tab	Control+Tab		Select next point in curve
Ctrl+Shift+Tab	Control+Shift+Tab		Select preview point in curve
D	D		Deselect point in curve
Ctrl+U	⌘+U		Toggle all Auto checkboxes
Ctrl+K	⌘+K		Preferences

Windows	Macintosh	Photoshop Elements 3	Photoshop CS2
Ctrl+A	⌘+A		In text field: Select all text In Filmstrip mode: Select all images
Ctrl+Alt+A or Alt+Select All button	⌘+Alt+A or Opt+Select All button		In Filmstrip mode: Select all rated images
Alt+Synchronize button	Opt+Synchronize button		In Filmstrip mode: Synchronize selected with previous settings (no dialog)

Index

Note to the Reader: Throughout this index **boldfaced** page numbers indicate primary discussions of a topic. *Italicized* page numbers indicate illustrations.

Tint control, 52, 72–73, *74*
    for white balance, 49
Tonal Width, for Smart Sharpen, 136–137
toolbar in Camera Raw, *29*
Tools menu (Bridge) > Photoshop > Batch, 102
transferring files, marking files to prevent, 6
transparency, saving in TIFF, 138
tungsten (incandescent) lighting, 48, *50*

U

underexposed image
    correcting, *53*, **53–54**, *54*
    histogram, *37*
Unsharp Mask, 68, 98, 134, **135**
USB (Universal Serial Bus), for camera connection
    to computer, 2
user input, preventing prompt when running
    Action, 103

V

View menu (Bridge) > Slideshow, 9
vignetting, **108–113**
    adding, **111–113**
    Lens tab to control, **109–110**

W

watermark, 98
web sites, JPEG files for, 138
White Balance tool, 32–33, *33*, **48–52**, *72*
    presets, **49**, *49*
    setting variations, *50*
White, in histogram, 38
white point, setting in Curves control, 115
Workflow settings, 33–34

X

XMP "sidecar" file, 123, 125

Y

Yellow, in histogram, 38

Z

ZIP compression, 138
zoom, for Luminance Smoothing, *74*
Zoom tool, **29–30**, *30*

INDEX

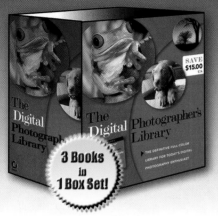
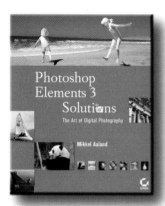

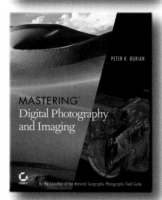

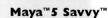
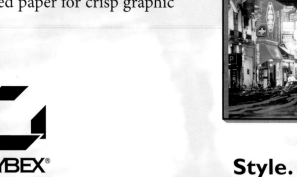